Creative
One-Piece Knitting

Creative
One-Piece Knitting

Elizabeth Vitek   Branka Kringas

Photography by Damien Kringas

Kangaroo Press

© Elizabeth Vitek and Branka Kringas 1993

First published in 1993 by Kangaroo Press Pty Ltd
3 Whitehall Road Kenthurst NSW 2156 Australia
P.O. Box 6125 Dural Delivery Centre NSW 2158 Australia
Typeset by G.T. Setters Pty Limited
Printed in Hong Kong by Colorcraft Ltd

ISBN 0 86417 503 5

Contents

Introduction

In the making of garments, there is an interesting difference between knitting and sewing. A sewn garment has to be cut from fabric before it is constructed and therefore there is a certain amount of waste. When a garment is knitted each piece is made to the exact finished shape. But there is another fascinating aspect to this: a sewn garment can be shaped only after it is cut from a piece of flat fabric, but a knitted garment can be shaped in any direction during the knitting process. This means that knitting can be done in three dimensions while sewing is limited to two.

In the past it was more common for garments to be knitted in one piece instead of being sewn together from a number of flat pieces. In recent years these techniques have been neglected.

In this book we hope to introduce enthusiastic knitters to some concepts in garment construction which may be new to them. All the garments are made in one piece; when the knitting is finished the garment is ready to wear, with the exception of some minor finishing touches.

Our aim in this book is also to cater to two types of knitters: those who wish to follow patterns using standard commercial yarns and those who would like to use different kinds of yarns such as silk, cotton, linen or hand-spun yarns, or who wish to make garments to non-standard measurements and find that printed patterns do not cater to their special needs. Therefore we have followed each pattern or group of patterns with a set of design instructions showing how the garments may be made to different specifications from those in the actual patterns.

We hope that this book will motivate our readers and free them to use their own creativity and imagination in choosing yarns, colours and textures to create their own individual designs.

Abbreviations

K: knit
P: purl
st: stitch
sl: slip
psso: pass the slipped stitch over
tog: together
rep: repeat
yfwd: yarn forward
st-st: stocking stitch†
inc: increase (by picking up a loop between the needle points and knitting into the back of it)
inc 1 P: increase (by picking up a loop between the needle points and purling into the back of it)
PM: place marker (take a short length of left-over yarn and knot it into a loop, then place it on the right-hand needle)
SM: slip marker (from left to right-hand needle point)

Special abbreviations for cable instructions, etc. are given with the relevant patterns.

Equipment

The equipment needed for knitting the garments in this book differs from standard knitting equipment in only one respect. Instead of pairs of straight needles, the garments are worked on circular needles. These consist of two rigid needle-ends (usually metal, but there are some available

---

† Stocking stitch: When knitting in rows, knit 1 row, purl 1 row. When knitting in rounds, knit every round.

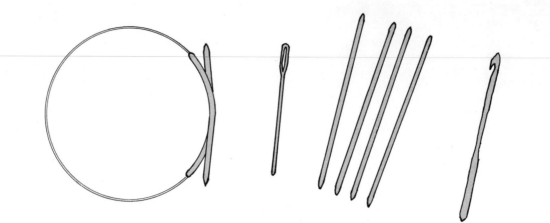

Basic equipment for one-piece knitting

in wood, plastic or bamboo) joined by a flexible nylon cord. The needles come in different lengths, the most generally useful measuring 80 cm. Although they were designed to be used for circular knitting, circular needles are equally useful for knitting back and forth in rows. The advantage is that the work can be neatly rolled up and put away without needle-ends sticking out and there is no problem of losing or breaking needles. Another advantage is that the stitches on the cord will not be stretched. When putting the work aside, the needle-ends should be pulled out away from the stitches so that the stitches are left on the cord. This will ensure a more even finish to the work. Using a circular needle and knitting in rounds also makes it possible to knit stripes in single rows without having to break off the yarn at the end of every row.

A circular needle of a given length must have a certain minimum number of stitches on it when working in rounds. Shorter circular needles are available, but they can be awkward to use; they are not practical when knitting sleeves, which have to be decreased down to fit the wrist. For this purpose sets of four double-pointed needles are used.

Some left-over yarn in a contrasting colour to your work will also be required. This is used for invisible casting on (see Special Techniques, page 11) and to make markers (by cutting off a short length, doubling it and knotting the ends together) which are used in many of the patterns. It may also be used for threading through stitches which are not in use and for placing pockets.

For measuring tension, a rigid ruler is more accurate than a tape measure. Better still is a tension square, which is available at good yarn shops. This is a hollow square with an inside measurement of exactly 10 cm. When it is placed over the sample on a flat surface, the stitches and rows can be easily counted without the use of pins.

Another useful piece of equipment is a row counter. Most of the patterns include instructions to work a specific number of rows and a row counter will help to keep the tally. Most row counters are designed to slip on the end of a straight needle, so they have to be used differently when working with a circular needle. One method is to tie the row counter to one of the loose ends at the beginning of the work or to a marker; it will then always be at hand when it is needed. If you are not using a row counter, mark every tenth row with a safety pin or a coloured thread.

Other necessary equipment includes:
  crochet hook
  stitch-holders
  cable needle
  tape measure
  wool needle (for darning in ends and grafting)
  scissors
  ruler (for checking tension)
  needle gauge

Table of Needle Sizes

The needle sizes specified in this book are metric. The following table shows the English and United States equivalents.

Metric (mm)	English	US
2.75	12	2
3	11	3
3.25	10	—
3.5	—	4
3.75	9	—
4	8	5
4.25	—	6
4.5	7	7
5	6	8
5.5	5	9
6	4	10
6.5	3	—

Handy Hints

About Yarns

The yarns specified in the patterns in this book are mostly standard 8-ply, 5-ply and 4-ply yarns. The specified tensions and recommended quantities have been worked out on readily available, good quality wool or cotton yarns. However, synthetic, specialty or hand-spun yarns may be used successfully, as long as they produce the specified tension. You will need to make a tension sample to make sure that the garment will fit properly (see Tension, page 10). If the number of stitches to 10 cm is more than the specified amount, use a larger needle; if there are fewer stitches to 10 cm, use a smaller needle.

Quantities: If you are using synthetic yarns, which are much lighter than wool yarns, you will not need as much as the amount given in the pattern (see next section).

Estimating Quantities

The quantity of yarn needed to complete a garment may be estimated reasonably accurately by doing some simple calculations based on your tension swatch. A small electronic calculator will help, and you will need a good set of metric kitchen scales to weigh your swatch. If your scales are not sensitive enough for such a small item, ask someone at a post office to weigh it for you on the letter scales. Alternatively, if you knit a swatch from a whole 50 gm ball of yarn, you will know that the swatch weighs 50 grams.

When you have measured your tension and obtained the number of stitches and rows over 10 cm, measure the area of the whole swatch. Then make a simplified diagram of your pattern as follows:

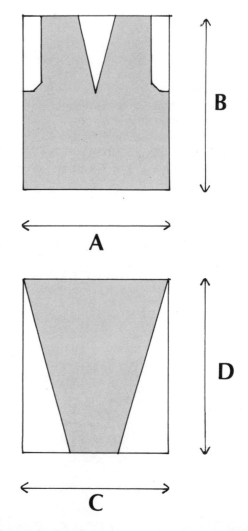

Estimating quantities

The upper diagram represents the front and back of the garment and the lower diagram the sleeves. A = half the bust or chest measurement; B = overall length; C = upper arm measurement; D = sleeve length. Calculate the area of each rectangle by multiplying A × B and C × D, add the results together and multiply them by two. Next, weigh the tension swatch. Divide the previously calculated area of the garment by the area of the swatch, then multiply the result by the weight of the tension swatch. The result should give the number of grams of yarn required to finish the garment, with allowance made for extras such as bands, pockets etc.

Example:
Bust or chest measurement, 90 cm (A = 45 cm). Overall length measurement (B), 65 cm. Upper arm measurement (C), 40 cm. Sleeve length (D), 48 cm. Area of garment, 45 × 65 (2925 square cm), plus 40 × 48 (1920 square cm) = 4845 square cm, multiplied by two = 9690 square cm.

Tension swatch measures 20 × 25 cm (500 square cm) and weighs 20 gm.

Area of garment (9690) divided by area of swatch (500) = 19.38; multiplied by the weight of the swatch (20) = 581.4 gm.

Round this out to 600 gm, which is twelve 50gm balls, and this should give a sufficient quantity to complete the garment.

An average sized sweater in 8-ply wool or similar weight will take approximately 600 to 700 gm. In lighter wool, such as 5-ply, 400 to 500 gm should be sufficient.

The body of a garment usually takes approximately the same amount of yarn as the two sleeves (less if it is close-fitting).

When buying yarn, ask for two extra 50 gm balls in the same dye lot to be put aside for you. They will then be available if you find that you need more than you estimated.

Tension

If you are making a garment from one of the patterns in this book, it will be absolutely necessary to work to the recommended tension to obtain the desired fit. To check your tension, cast on 40 sts in the specified yarn on the specified needles. Work 50 rows in st-st, cast off. Press the sample (if the finished garment is to be pressed) and leave it for twenty-four hours before measuring it. Using a rigid ruler or a tension square (see Equipment, page 8) rather than a tape measure, measure 10 cm across the work and mark with pins. Turn the sample around and measure 10 cm from top to bottom. Mark again with pins. Carefully count the stitches and rows between the pins and compare with the tension recommended in the pattern. If you have more stitches than you should your tension is too tight. Try another sample on larger needles. If you have not enough stitches your tension is too loose. Try again on smaller needles. These experiments can be made all on the one sample, with a purl row between each as a marker.

If you wish to use the alternative instructions for making your own version of one of the designs, perhaps with different yarn from that specified in the pattern or with different measurements, you will first need to make a tension sample according to these instructions in the yarn which you have chosen and with appropriate sized needles. If the yarn is very thick it will be sufficient to cast on a smaller number of stitches and work a smaller number of rows. The object is to obtain a sample measuring not less than 15 × 15 cm. Experiment with different sized needles, working 15 cm with each size with a purl row between to indicate a

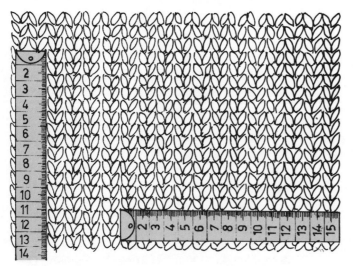

Measuring tension

change of needle size, until you decide which size of needle gives the effect you want. Work the sample in the stitch you intend to use for the main area of the garment. If you are using a mixture of yarns of different plies and textures, knit the sample with all of them, 15 cm each and in the same sample. Make sure that the different plies are not too different from the main yarn and work thinner yarns in textured stitches, thicker yarns in stocking stitch. When working out the calculations for the design, use the tension of the main yarn.

When you have your final tension sample, made with the correct needles and in the stitch you wish to use, measure off 10 cm as described above and count the number of stitches. Dividing this number of stitches by 10 will give the number of stitches in 1 cm (for example, 17 sts to 10 cm equals 1.7 sts to 1 cm).

Taking Measurements

If you wish to make one of our designs to your own specifications instead of using the worked-out pattern, you will need to take accurate measurements. The final fit of the garment will depend on how carefully these measurements are taken. The measurements you will need are chest, shoulders, upper arm, sleeve length, wrist and overall length.

For the chest, measure loosely around the widest part. An extra 10 cm should then be added to give a comfortable fit. If the hips are larger than the chest, the hip measurement may be used instead.

Measure the shoulders across the back from point of one shoulder to the point of the other. Use a wider measure if a slightly dropped shoulder line is desired. If you are making one of the striped-side sweater designs, make this measurement somewhat narrower.

For the upper arm, take the tape measure from the top of the shoulder under the arm and back to the top of the shoulder. This should be a close measurement, but you may add more if a really loose fit is required. If you measure directly around the upper arm itself, the sleeve will be too tight.

Measure the wrist with two fingers under the tape. Carry the tape rather loosely around the wrist.

Overall length is measured from the shoulder to the point where you wish the garment to finish.

Special Techniques

Invisible Casting On

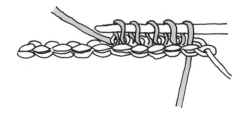

Invisible casting on

Using a crochet hook of a similar size to the knitting needles to be used and a small quantity of left-over yarn, crochet a chain four or five stitches longer than the required number of cast-on stitches. With the yarn you are using for the garment, pick up the necessary number of stitches by inserting the needle into the back loop of each stitch in the chain. Leave the chain in place while continuing the work. When the time comes to knit these stitches in the other direction, with the right side of the work facing pick up the required number of stitches from the loops of the previous casting on. When it is no longer needed, remove the chain by drawing the end through the last loop and gently pulling it undone.

Casting On by the Thumb Method

The thumb method of casting on is normally used when the cast-on stitches are to be joined into a round, either on double-pointed or circular needles.

Make a loop in the yarn at a point approximately three times the circumference of the casting on plus a few centimetres and place it on the right-hand needle point. To estimate the required length more accurately, cast on 10 or 20 sts, then undo them and measure the yarn used. Use this measurement to calculate the length needed for the required number of stitches to be cast on. With this 'tail' of yarn, make a loop over the left thumb and knit it on to the right-hand needle. Continue in this manner until the required number of stitches is cast on. The first stitch cast on will thus be at the other end of the needle (or needles). Begin the first round by working on from this stitch after making sure that there is no twist in the casting on.

Turning

When making short-row shapings for shoulders, the pattern instructions are to knit a number of stitches

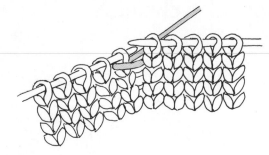

Turning

and turn. In order to make these shapings invisible, work the turnings as follows: Knit the required number of stitches, yarn front, slip the next stitch, yarn back and slip the stitch back again, then turn. When knitting past this point on the next row, pick up the loop thus made around the stitch and knit it together with the stitch.

Grafting

This method may be used to join together two rows of stitches (such as back and front shoulders) without the appearance of a seam. Hold the needles containing the back and front stitches in the left hand, wrong sides together. Break off the yarn, leaving a sufficient length for the grafting, and thread it on a wool needle. Take the wool needle through the first stitch on the front needle purlwise and leave the stitch on the knitting needle. Take the wool needle under the front needle and through the first stitch on the back needle knitwise and leave the stitch on the knitting needle. Take the wool needle through the first stitch on the front needle knitwise and slip it off. Take the wool needle through the second stitch on the front needle purlwise and leave it on. Take the wool needle under the front needle and through the first stitch on the back needle purlwise and slip it off. Take the wool needle through the second stitch on the front needle knitwise and leave it on. Continue in this manner until all the stitches are grafted.

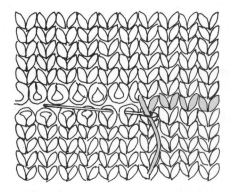

Grafting

Joining Shoulders

Several methods may be used for joining the shoulders of a garment which has been worked from the bottom up.

1. The stitches may be grafted together (see Grafting above).

2. The back and front stitches may be cast off together to give a more textured effect:

(a) For a ridged effect, hold the two needles with the back shoulder stitches and the front shoulder stitches side by side in the left hand, wrong sides together. Using a third needle, knit the first stitches on the front and back needles together, then knit the second stitches and cast off the first. Continue in this manner until all the stitches are cast off. For a seamed effect, hold the needles with right sides together.

(b) For a flatter effect, starting on the left side, hold the needle with the front shoulder stitches in the left hand and the needle with the back shoulder stitches in the right hand. Slip the first stitch from the right-hand needle to the left-hand needle and K 2 tog. *Slip 2 sts from right-hand needle to left-hand needle and K 3 tog.* Rep from * to * to end of shoulder stitches. For the right side, hold the needle with the back shoulder stitches in the left hand, the needle with the front shoulder stitches in the right hand. Work as for left side, but K 3 tog through back of loops.

Joining Yarns

The most usual method of joining in a new ball of yarn is to do it at the end of a row. However, this is not possible when knitting in rounds on a circular needle. In order to make a neat join which will not be visible the yarn should be spliced.

To do this, take the end of the yarn to be joined to the new ball and separate the strands. Break off about 4 or 5 cm from half the strands. Do the same with the end of the new ball, then lay the remaining strands of each end of yarn alongside the remaining strands of the other in the palm of your hand. Moisten your palms and rub them lightly together over the yarn. The result should be a completely invisible join which is as strong as the rest of the yarn.

If there are only three strands in the yarn, break off one strand from one end and two from the other.

This method is effective for joining wool yarns, but not for synthetic yarns or wool-synthetic mixes. When joining in a new ball of this kind of yarn, leave a tail of yarn about 8 to 10 cm long on both the old ball and the new ball. Work a few rounds, then darn in the tails of yarn by taking a few slip sts along the back of the work, taking care not to pull the yarn too tight.

Multi-coloured or Picture Knitting in the Round

There are two different methods of working with more than one colour at a time. The first and by far the older technique is the Fair Isle method, where geometrical designs are worked in only a few stitches of any one colour at a time, the colours being repeated across the row or round. In this case, the colours not being worked are carried behind the stitches worked with the other yarn. This means that the yarn is always taken to the end of the row or round and is ready for use in the next row or round.

The second method of multi-coloured knitting is called 'picture knitting'; and it requires larger blocks of colours to be worked in a given area of the knitting. The yarn not in use cannot be carried behind the stitches of the next colour because the area is too large. The easiest way of handling the several different yarns which may be needed is to wind small quantities on to plastic yarn bobbins, which are held at the back of the work when not in use. (If the areas of different colours are very large this may not be necessary.) When changing from one colour to another the yarns are twisted around each other so that there are no holes in the work.

Because the colours are left in place when the next colour is being worked, it is necessary to work back and forth when doing picture knitting. However, the work can still be done seamlessly. Here are two methods of doing this:

1. The first method is to use two circular needles. Following the diagram, divide the round into two convenient halves at points A and B where the colours join. Using the first needle, K from A to B.

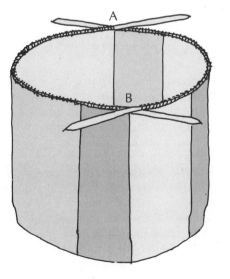

Using the second needle, P from A to B. Twist yarns together. Using the first needle, P from B to A. Using the second needle, K from B to A. Always remember to twist the yarns together when changing from one colour to another. If it is necessary to change the position of the join at the end of the two needles, the necessary number of stitches may be worked from one needle to the other. In most cases there will be more than two colours to a round. In this case, more than one colour can be carried on one needle. Each needle need not have the same number of stitches as the other.

2. If there is an area of colour in your design which consists of less than 10 sts, locate point A at the beginning of this area and point B at the end of it. Begin the round at point A, knit through point B to point A. Slip the sts from A to B back on to the left-hand needle point, then purl from B through A back to B. Slip the sts from B to A back on to the left-hand needle point and repeat the process.

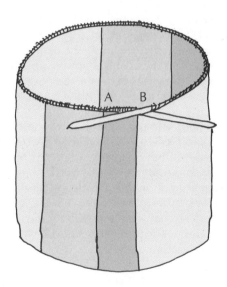

Picking Up Stitches

To pick up stitches along the edge of a piece of work when the same-sized needles are being used, pick up two stitches to every three rows. If a smaller sized needle is being used (i.e. for a ribbed band), pick up one stitch for every row along a straight edge and approximately three stitches for four rows along a shaped edge.

To pick up a stitch, insert the needle between the first and second stitch of the row. If a flatter effect is required and the edge of the work is neat, insert the needle into the centre of the last stitch of the row.

A Note About Sleeves

The sleeves in most of these patterns are knitted from the top down. The first 5 cm have no shaping; after that they are shaped by decreasing every 4th or 6th round. The shapings are designed to end just above the cuff. These shapings have been designed to fit a standard length of sleeve, as shown on the patterns.

Before commencing a sleeve, check your sleeve length against the sleeve length given in the pattern. If your arm is longer than the given measurement, add the extra length at the top of the sleeve before beginning the shaping. If your arm is shorter, work the sleeve until it will fit your arm minus 5 cm for the cuff. You will end up with a few more sts than have been specified for the end of the sleeve. These sts can be taken off by decreasing in the last row above the cuff.

Placing Buttonholes

The bands on the cardigans in this book are worked by picking up stitches along the edges, not by making a long strip. Because the length of the garments is not specified, it is not possible to give an exact number of sts between each buttonhole.

When picking up the sts for the band, place a marker at the point where the neck shaping begins. When you come to the buttonhole row, count the sts from the lower edge to the marker. Subtract the total number of buttonhole sts from this number, then subtract the number of sts given in the pattern before the first buttonhole. Divide the result by the number of buttons minus one. This will give the number of sts between the buttonholes. If the number does not divide evenly adjust it with a few sts after the last buttonhole.

Example: Number of sts in band to neck shaping = 126; number of buttons = 6; number of sts per buttonhole = 3; number of sts before 1st buttonhole = 4. 126 minus 4 = 122; subtract 18 sts for buttonholes = 104; divide 104 by 5 = 20 and 4 over. There will then be 20 sts between each buttonhole and 4 after the last one.

Finishing Touches

The best feature of one-piece knitting is that when the last stitch has been knitted the garment is virtually ready to wear. However, some finishing touches are needed. In the first place, the ends of the yarn must be neatly darned in to the back of the work. This can be made even easier if it is done progressively as the work continues. After casting off the last stitch, or at any point in the work where the yarn is to be broken off and rejoined in another place, leave an end about 10 cm long. Thread this end on to a wool needle and take six or eight stitches in a straight line on the back of the work.

When garments are knitted from the top down, it is essential that the cast-off edges are sufficiently elastic. If the last rows are in rib, the casting off must also be in rib. This means that, when casting off, all the knit stitches should be knitted and all the purl stitches purled. In order to cast off more loosely, use the following method: Work 2 sts, pass the first stitch over the second and leave it on the left-hand needle point. Work the next stitch and drop both stitches off the needle together.

To finish the casting off neatly, when the last stitch is cast off break off the yarn and pull the last stitch out. Thread the end of yarn on to a wool needle. Take the needle under the first cast-off stitch from front to back, then down through the last cast-off stitch. Finish off by taking a few slip stitches at the back of the work before cutting off the end of yarn.

To Press or Not to Press?

This will be a decision for the individual in most cases. Some people like hand-knitted garments to be well pressed; others prefer them to emphasise the texture.

There are some situations where pressing is definitely not indicated. Firstly, it may not be recommended for some synthetic yarns. Instructions on pressing will normally be found on the ball band. Secondly, highly textured patterns such as Arans are more attractive if they are unpressed.

Fitting Garments

When garments are made in one piece, it is possible to check the fit while the work is in progress. If a garment is being worked from the top, it may be tried on for size at a stage when one or both sleeves have been completed. Take a long length of contrasting yarn on a wool needle and thread it through all the body stitches. Make sure it is long enough for the body to be stretched out fully without losing any of the stitches. Alternatively, half the sts may be threaded on to a second circular needle of the same or smaller size.

In this way the length of the garment can be determined while it is being fitted on the wearer.

Recycling Yarn

Old or outdated garments need not be discarded; they can be remade into something new and different. The yarn from several different garments can be combined into an attractive design of stripes or other multi-coloured patterns.

When the yarn is unravelled it will have to be dekinked before reuse. While you are unravelling it, wind it into skeins of a manageable length, taking care not to make the skeins too big. Tie each skein loosely in several places with cotton tape or narrow strips of cloth. Wash the yarn, using a good wool-washing liquid, and hang it to dry. When it is thoroughly dry, wind it into balls.

Another method of dekinking the yarn is to wind it onto cardboard cylinders (such as those from rolls of aluminium foil or plastic wrap), spray it with a little water and put it in a microwave oven for 30 seconds on high. Alternatively the yarn may be wound onto a facecloth or a small piece of towelling wrung out in hot water, and placed in the microwave to dry.

Striped-side Sweater in 5-ply

Illustrated on facing page

This comfortable sweater features stripes of contrasting colour and texture at each side. The central portions of the front and back are knitted in one piece; the side panels are constructed from stitches knitted up along the sides of this piece and the sleeves are a continuation of the side panels.

Fits chest size (cm)

A	B	C	D	E	F	G
80	85	**90**	95	**100**	105	**110**

Measures (cm)

90	95	**100**	105	**110**	115	**120**

Sleeve length, underarm to wrist (cm)

42	44	**45**	47	**48**	49	50

Materials

50 gm balls of 5-ply yarn
Main colour (M): **9**: 10: **11**: 12: **12**: 13: **14** balls
Contrast (C): 2 balls
80 cm circular needles and sets of four double-pointed needles in sizes 3.75 mm and 3 mm
6 small buttons
Small quantity of left-over yarn
Stitch-holder

Tension

26 sts and 36 rows to 10 cm, measured over stocking stitch, using 3.75 mm needles.

INSTRUCTIONS

The work begins with the back of the centre panel, which is worked in one piece.

Using 3.75 mm circular needle invisibly cast on **84**: 92: **96**: 104: **110**: 118: **122** sts. Beginning with a K row, work in st-st until back measures desired length from lower edge to shoulder minus 5 cm, ending with a P row.

Shape back shoulders

1st row: K **70**: 76: **80**: 86: **92**: 98: **102**, turn (see Special Techniques, page 11).
2nd row: P **56**: 60: **64**: 68: **74**: 78: **82**, turn.
3rd row: K **63**: 68: **72**: 77: **83**: 88: **92**, turn.
4th row: P **70**: 76: **80**: 86: **92**: 98: **102**, turn.
5th row: K to end.
6th row: P.

Shape front shoulders

1st row: K **21**: 23: **24**: 26: **27**: 29: **30** (right side). Place next **42**: 46: **48**: 52: **56**: 60: **62** sts on a stitch-holder. Join in a second ball of yarn, K **7**: 7: **8**: 8: **9**: 9: **10** (left side), turn.
2nd row: P back across left side, P **7**: 7: **8**: 8: **9**: 9: **10** on right side, turn.
3rd row: K back across right side, K **14**: 16: **16**: 18: **18**: 20: **20** on left side, turn.
4th row: P back across left side, P **14**: 16: **16**: 18: **18**: 20: **20** on right side, turn.
5th row: K back across right side, K to end of left side.
6th row: P left and right sides.

Continue working without shaping until neck edge measures 5 cm, ending with a wrong-side row.

Inc 1 st at neck edge in next and every alternate row **11**: 11: **12**: 13: **14**: 15: **15** times (**32**: 34: **36**: 39: **41**: 44: **45** sts each side).

Striped-side sweater in 5-ply (facing page)

Striped-side sweater in 8-ply (page 20)

Sweater with 'hands' pattern (page 22)

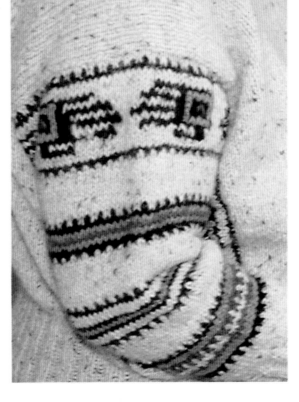

Detail of 'hands' pattern

18

Next row: P across left side, invisibly cast on **7**: 9: **9**: 10: **11**: 12: **13** sts. P across right side.
Next row: K across right side, invisibly cast on **7**: 9: **9**: 10: **11**: 12: **13** sts. K across left side.

Continue working in st-st for **47**: 53: **55**: 61: **67**: 73: **77** more rows.
Next row: K across right side. Using same ball of yarn, cast on 6 sts and K across left side. Break off yarn from left side (**84**: 92: **96**: 104: **110**: 118: **122** sts).

Continue working in st-st until front measures the same as the back. Thread sts on a length of left-over yarn.

Side panels

Using 3.75 mm circular needle and beginning at lower left-hand edge of front, with right side of work facing, pick up two stitches for every three rows along side edge of front and back.

Work 5 rows in st-st.
Change to C and K 2 rows.
Change to M and work 2 rows in st-st.
Change to C and work 6 rows in moss stitch.†
Change to M and work 2 rows in st-st.
Change to C and K 2 rows. Break off C.
Change to M and work 4 rows in st-st. Before working the 3rd row, count the sts. When working the 3rd row, place a marker when half the sts have been worked, then work **67**: 70: **73**: 74: **74**: 77: **77** sts, PM, work to end.
4th row: Work **67**: 70: **73**: 74: **74**: 77: **77** sts past the half-way marker and place another marker. The half-way marker may then be removed (**134**: 140: **146**: 148: **148**: 154: **154** between markers).

Join sides together from lower end of front and back to markers, either by grafting the sts (see Special Techniques, page 11) or by using method 2(b) described in the Joining Shoulders section of Special Techniques.

Sleeves

Place the remaining **134**: 140: **146**: 148: **148**: 154: **154** sts onto three 3.75 mm double-pointed needles, distributing the sts evenly.

K 1 round.
Next round: K 1, K 2 tog, K to last 3 sts, sl 1, K 1, psso, K 1. K 1 round.

Rep these 2 rounds 9 times, then decrease in the same manner every 4th round until **60**: 62: **66**: 64: **64**: 68: **68** sts remain.

---

†Moss stitch: 1st row: (K 1, P 1) to end. If this row ends with a K st, work 2nd row as 1st row. If the last st of the 1st row is a P st, begin the 2nd row with P 1. Continue in this manner, beginning each row with the same st as the last st of the previous row.

*Work **2**: 2: **2**: 2: **4**: 4: **4** rounds without shaping.
Change to C and K 1 round.
Next round: P 1, P 2 tog, P to last 3 sts, P 2 tog, P 1. Change to M.*
Rep from * to * once. Break off C.
Work 3 rounds without shaping.
Next round: Decrease **4**: 2: **4**: 0: **0**: 0: **0** sts evenly over round (**52**: 56: **58**: 60: **60**: 64: **64** sts).

Change to 3 mm double-pointed needles and work 5 cm in K 1, P 1 rib. Cast off loosely in rib.
Work right side and sleeve to correspond.

Basque

Using 3 mm circular needle, beginning at left-hand lower edge of centre back section, knit up **84**: 92: **96**: 104: **110**: 118: **122** sts from invisible casting on, then knit up **33**: 32: **34**: 33: **33**: 32: **34** sts along edge of right side panel, **84**: 92: **96**: 104: **110**: 118: **122** sts from lower edge of front section, and **33**: 32: **34**: 33: **33**: 32: **34** sts along edge of left side panel (**234**: 248: **260**: 274: **286**: 300: **312** sts).

Work 5 cm in K 1, P 1 rib. Cast off loosely in rib.

Neckband

Using 3 mm circular needle, knit up **7**: 9: **9**: 10: **11**: 12: **13** sts from invisible casting on at right-hand neck edge, then knit up **30**: 30: **32**: 33: **35**: 36: **36** sts evenly up right front, **42**: 46: **48**: 52: **56**: 60: **62** sts from stitch-holder, **30**: 30: **32**: 33: **35**: 36: **36** sts evenly down left front and **7**: 9: **9**: 10: **11**: 12: **13** sts from invisible casting on at left-hand neck edge (**132**: 142: **148**: 158: **170**: 180: **186** sts).

Work 8 rows in K 1, P 1 rib. Cast off loosely in rib.

Left front band

Using 3 mm needle, with right side facing and beginning at cast-off edge of neckband, knit up **53**: 59: **61**: 67: **73**: 79: **83** sts evenly down left side of front opening.
1st row: K 1, P 1 to end.
2nd row: K 2, (P 1, K 1) to last st, K 1.

Rep these 2 rows 3 times. Cast off loosely in rib.
Work right front band to correspond, working buttonholes in 4th row as follows: Rib **4**: 5: **6**: 3: **4**: 5: **4**, *yfwd, K 2 tog, rib **7**: 8: **8**: 10: **11**: 12: **13***, rep from * to * 4 times, yfwd, K 2 tog, rib **2**: 2: **3**: 2: **2**: 2: **2**.

Making up

Darn in ends. Stitch down ends of front band to casting on. Sew on buttons. Press if desired.

Striped-side Sweater in 8-ply

Illustrated on page 16

This sweater is constructed in the same manner as the 5-ply Striped-side Sweater, but with a V-neck.

Fits chest size (cm)

A	B	C	D	E	F	G
80	85	**90**	95	**100**	105	**110**

Measures (cm)

90	95	**100**	105	**110**	115	**120**

Sleeve length, underarm to wrist (cm)

42	44	**45**	47	**48**	49	**50**

Materials

50 gm balls of 8-ply yarn
Main colour (M): **11**: 12: **12**: 13: **14**: 15: **16** balls
Contrast (C): 2 balls
80 cm circular needles and sets of four double-pointed needles in sizes 4 mm and 3.25 mm
Small quantity of left-over yarn
Stitch-holder

Tension

22 sts and 30 rows to 10 cm, measured over stocking stitch, using 4 mm needles.

INSTRUCTIONS

The work begins with the centre panel, which is worked in one piece from the bottom of the back.

Using 4 mm circular needle invisibly cast on **72**: 78: **84**: 88: **94**: 100: **106** sts. Beginning with a K row, work in st-st until back measures desired length from lower edge to shoulder minus 5 cm, ending with a P row.

Shape back shoulders

1st row: K **60**: 66: **70**: 74: **78**: 84: **88**, turn (see Special Techniques, page 11).
2nd row: P **48**: 54: **56**: 60: **62**: 68: **70**, turn.
3rd row: K **54**: 60: **63**: 67: **70**: 76: **79**, turn.
4th row: P **60**: 66: **70**: 74: **78**: 84: **88**, turn.
5th row: K to end.
6th row: P.

Shape front shoulders

1st row: K **18**: 19: **21**: 22: **23**: 25: **26** (right side). Place next **36**: 40: **42**: 44: **48**: 50: **54** sts on a stitch-holder. Join in a second ball of yarn, K **6**: 7: **7**: 8: **7**: 9: **8** (left side), turn.
2nd row: P back across left side, P **6**: 7: **7**: 8: **7**: 9: **8** on right side, turn.
3rd row: K back across right side, K **12**: 12: **14**: 14: **16**: 16: **18** on left side, turn.
4th row: P back across left side, P **12**: 12: **14**: 14: **16**: 16: **18** on right side, turn.
5th row: K back across right front, K to end of left front.
6th row: P left and right front.
7th row: K to last st of right front, inc 1, K 1. On left front, K 1, inc 1, K to end.

Continue working in st-st, increasing every 4th row, as in 7th row, until there are **36**: 39: **42**: 44: **47**: 50: **53** sts on each side.

Work 3 more rows, then join the two fronts together by working right and left fronts with the same ball of yarn. Break off yarn from left front.

Continue working in st-st until front measures the same as the back. Thread sts on a length of left-over yarn.

Side panels

Using 4 mm circular needle and beginning at lower left-hand edge of front, with right side of work facing, pick up two stitches for every three rows along side edge of front and back.

Work 2 rows in st-st.

Change to C and work 6 rows.

Change to M and work 2 rows.

Change to C and work 4 rows.

Change to M and work 2 rows.

Change to C and work 2 rows. Break off C.

Change to M and work 2 rows. Before working these rows, count the sts. When working the 1st row, place a marker when half the sts have been worked, then work **59**: 61: **63**: 64: **65**: 68: **68**, PM, work to end.

2nd row: Work **59**: 61: **63**: 64: **65**: 68: **68** sts past the half-way marker and place another marker. The half-way marker may then be removed (**118**: 122: **126**: 128: **130**: 136: **136** sts).

Join sides together from lower end of front and back to markers, either by grafting the sts (see Special Techniques, page 11) or by using method 2(b) described in the 'Joining Shoulders' section of Special Techniques.

Sleeves

Place the remaining **118**: 122: **126**: 128: **130**: 136: **136** sts onto three 4 mm double-pointed needles, distributing the sts evenly. K 1 round.

Next round: K 1, K 2 tog, K to last 3 sts, sl 1, K 1, psso, K 1. K 1 round.

Rep these 2 rounds 9 times, then decrease in the same manner every 4th round until **50**: 50: **52**: 52: **52**: 56: **56** sts remain.

Work 3 rounds without shaping.

Next round: Decrease **6**: 6: **4**: 4: **0**: 0: **0** sts evenly over round (**44**: 44: **48**: 48: **52**: 56: **56** sts).

Change to 3.25 mm double-pointed needles and work 5 cm in K 2, P 2 rib. Cast off loosely in rib.

Work right side and sleeve to correspond.

Basque

Using 3.25 mm circular needle, beginning at left-hand lower edge of centre back section, knit up **72**: 78: **84**: 88: **94**: 100: **106** sts from invisible casting on, then knit up **26**: 26: **26**: 28: **26**: 26: **26** sts along edge of right side panel, **72**: 78: **84**: 88: **94**: 100: **106** sts from lower edge of front section, and **26**: 26: **26**: 28: **26**: 26: **26** sts along edge of left side panel (**196**: 208: **220**: 232: **240**: 252: **264** sts).

Work 5 cm in K 2, P 2 rib. Cast off loosely in rib.

Neckband

Using 3.25 mm double-pointed needles, with right side of work facing, join in yarn at right-hand end of back neck and knit up **36**: 40: **42**: 44: **48**: 50: **54** sts from stitch-holder. Knit up **56**: 64: **68**: 72: **76**: 80: **86** sts evenly along left front, placing a marker before the last 2 sts, then knit up **56**: 64: **66**: 68: **76**: 78: **84** sts along right front (**148**: 168: **176**: 184: **200**: 208: **224** sts). Divide sts on to 3 needles.

1st round: Sizes **A, B, D, E** and **G**: (P 2, K 2) to end. Sizes **C** and **F**: (K 2, P 2) to end.

*2nd round: Sizes **A, B, D, E** and **G**: (P 2, K 2) to 2 sts before marker, P 2 tog, SM, K 2, P 2 tog, K 2, (P 2, K 2) to end. Sizes **C** and **F**: (K 2, P 2) to 4 sts before marker, K 2, P 2 tog, SM, K 2, P 2 tog, (K 2, P 2) to end.

3rd round: Sizes **A, B, D, E** and **G**: (P 2, K 2) to 5 sts before marker, P 2, K 1, sl 1, K 1, psso, SM, K 2, K 2 tog, K 1, (P 2, K 2) to end. Sizes **C** and **F**: (K 2, P 2) to 3 sts before marker, K 1, sl 1, K 1, psso, SM, K 2 tog, K 1, P 2, (K 2, P 2) to end.

4th round: Sizes **A, B, D, E** and **G**: (P 2, K 2) to 4 sts before marker, P 2, sl 1, K 1, psso, SM, K 2, K 2 tog, (P 2, K 2) to end. Sizes **C** and **F**: (K 2, P 2) to 2 sts before marker, sl 1, K 1, psso, SM, K 2, K 2 tog, P 2, (K 2, P 2) to end.

5th round: Sizes **A, B, D, E** and **G**: (P 2, K 2) to 3 sts before marker, P 1, P 2 tog, SM, K 2, P 2 tog, P 1, K 2, (P 2, K 2) to end. Sizes **C** and **F**: (K 2, P 2) to 5 sts before marker, K 2, P 1, P 2 tog, SM, K 2, P 2 tog, P 1, (K 2, P 2) to end.*

Rep from * to * once. Cast off loosely in rib.

Making up

Darn in ends. Press if desired.

Sweater with 'Hands' Pattern

Illustrated on page 18

This round-necked sweater is constructed in a similar manner to the striped-side sweaters but features a design of stylised hands on the side panels, as well as an interesting striped design on the sleeves. It is made in 8-ply yarn on larger needles.

Fits chest size (cm)

A	B	C	D	E	F
85	90	**95**	100	**105**	110

Measures (cm)

95	100	**105**	110	**115**	120

Sleeve length, underarm to wrist (cm)

44	45	**47**	48	**49**	50

Materials

50 gm balls of 8-ply yarn
Main colour (M): **11**: 11: **12**: 12: **13**: 14 balls
1 ball each of 4 contrasting colours (C1 to C4).

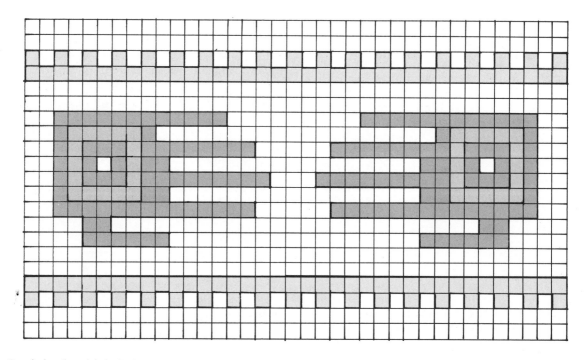

Graph for 'hands' design'

80 cm circular needles and sets of four double-pointed needles in sizes 5 mm and 4 mm
Small quantity of left-over yarn
Stitch-holder

Tension

19 sts and 26 rows to 10 cm, measured over stocking stitch, using 4 mm needles.

INSTRUCTIONS

The work begins with the centre panel, which is worked in one piece from the bottom of the back.

Using 5 mm circular needle invisibly cast on **76**: 82: **86**: 90: **96**: 100 sts. Beginning with a K row, work in st-st until back measures **54**: 55: **55**: 56: **56**: 57 cm, ending with a P row.

Shape back shoulders

1st row: K **60**: 64: **68**: 70: **74**: 78, turn (see Special Techniques, page 11).
2nd row: P **44**: 46: **50**: 50: **52**: 56, turn.
3rd row: K **52**: 55: **59**: 60: **63**: 67, turn.
4th row: P **60**: 64: **68**: 70: **74**: 78, turn.
5th row: K to end.
6th row: P.

Shape front shoulders

1st row: K **25**: 27: **28**: 30: **31**: 33 (right side). Place next **26**: 28: **30**: 30: **32**: 34 sts on a stitch-holder. Join in a second ball of yarn, K **9**: 9: **10**: 10: **10**: 11 (left side), turn.
2nd row: P back across left side, P **9**: 9: **10**: 10: **10**: 11 on right side, turn.
3rd row: K back across right side, K **16**: 18: **18**: 20: **22**: 22 on left side, turn.
4th row: P back across left side, P **16**: 18: **18**: 20: **22**: 22 on right side, turn.
5th row: K back across right front, K to end of left front.
6th row: P left and right front.

Continue working without shaping until neck edge measures 5 cm, ending with a wrong-side row.

Inc 1 st at neck edge in next and every alternate row **6**: 7: **7**: 7: **8**: 8 times (**25**: 27: **28**: 30: **32**: 33 sts). P 1 row then break off yarn from left side.
Next row: K across right side, invisibly cast on **14**: 14: **16**: 16: **16**: 18 sts, K across left side.

Continue working in st-st until front measures the same as the back. Thread sts on a length of left-over yarn.

Side panels

Using 5 mm circular needle and beginning at lower left-hand edge of front, with right side of work facing, pick up **103**: 104: **104**: 106: **106**: 108 sts up side of front, PM, then pick up **103**: 104: **104**: 106: **106**: 108 sts down side of back.
1st row: (P 1 in M, P 1 in C1) to end.
2nd row: Using C1, K.
3rd row: Using M, P.
4th row: Using M, K.
5th to 13th rows: Work in in st-st, work 1st **6**: 7: **7**: 6: **6**: 7 sts in M, then follow the chart for the hand pattern (15 sts, 5 hands each side), using C2, C3 and C4. Work **4**: 4: **4**: 5: **5**: 5 sts between each pattern repeat and **6**: 6: **6**: 5: **5**: 6 sts between the end of the 5th hand and the marker. SM, then work the back to correspond, reversing the hand pattern so that the fingers point upwards.
14th row: Using M, K.
15th row: Using M, P.
16th row: Using C1, K.
17th row: (P 1 in M, P 1 in C1) to end.

Slip **49**: 48: **47**: 49: **47**: 49 sts on to a separate needle. Hold this needle alongside the circular needle. Using a third 5 mm needle and M, K tog the first st on the front and back needle, then K tog the next st. Pass the first st over the second to cast off. Repeat this process until **49**: 48: **47**: 49: **47**: 49 sts have been cast off.

Sleeves

Place the remaining **108**: 112: **114**: 114: **118**: 118 sts onto three 5 mm double-pointed needles, distributing the sts evenly. K 1 round.

While working the sleeve shaping as described below, work the striped pattern as follows:
Work **13**: 14: **17**: 18: **19**: 21 rounds in M.
1st round: Work alternate sts in M and C2.
2nd round: Work in C2.
3rd round: Work in C3.
4th round: Work in C4.
5th round: Work in C3.
6th round: Work in C2.
7th round: Work alternate sts in M and C2
Work 12 rounds in M.
20th round: Work alternate sts in M and C1.
21st round: Work in C1.
Work 2 rounds in M.
24th round: Work in C1.
25th round: Work in C3.
26th round: Work in C1.
Work 2 rounds in M.
29th round: Work in C1.
30th round: Work alternate sts in M and C1.
Work 12 rounds in M.

43rd round: Work alternate sts in M and C2.
44th round: Work in C2.
Work 2 rounds in C3.
47th round: Work in C4.
48th round: Work alternate sts in M and C4.
49th round: Work in M.
50th round: Work alternate sts in M and C4.
51st round: Work in C4.
Work 2 rounds in C3.
54th round: Work in C2.
55th round: Work alternate sts in M and C2.
Complete sleeve in M.

While working the striped pattern as described above, work the sleeve shaping as follows:
Next round: K 1, K 2 tog, K to last 3 sts, sl 1, K 1, psso, K 1. K 1 round.

Rep these 2 rounds 9 times, then decrease in the same manner every 4th round until **46**: 50: **48**: 48: **52**: 48 sts remain.

Work 3 rounds without shaping.
Next round: Decrease **6**: 10: **8**: 4: **8**: 0 sts evenly over round (**40**: 40: **40**: 44: **44**: 48 sts).

Change to 4 mm double-pointed needles and work 5 cm in K 2, P 2 rib. Cast off loosely in rib.

Work right side and sleeve to correspond.

Basque

Using 4 mm circular needle, beginning at left-hand lower edge of centre back section, knit up **76**: 82: **86**: 90: **96**: 100 sts from invisible casting on, then knit up 14 sts along edge of right side panel, **76**: 82: **86**: 90: **96**: 100 sts from lower edge of front section, and 14 sts along edge of left side panel (**180**: 192: **200**: 208: **220**: 228 sts).

Work 5 cm in K 2, P 2 rib. Cast off loosely in rib.

Neckband

Using 4 mm double-pointed needles, with right side of work facing, join in yarn at right-hand end of back neck and knit up **26**: 28: **30**: 30: **32**: 34 sts from stitch-holder. Knit up **20**: 21: **21**: 21: **22**: 22 sts evenly along left front, **14**: 14: **16**: 16: **16**: 18 sts from centre front invisible casting on, then knit up **20**: 21: **21**: 21: **22**: 22 sts along right front (**80**: 84: **88**: 88: **92**: 96 sts). Divide sts on to 3 needles.

Work 8 rows in K 2, P 2 rib. Cast off loosely in rib.

Making up

Darn in ends. Press if desired.

Striped-side Sweater

First make a tension sample (see Tension, page 10) and take measurements (see Taking Measurements, page 11).

Back

From the shoulder measurement, calculate the number of sts needed for the central panel. The shoulder measurement for this design should be approximately 5 cm narrower than for an ordinary sweater.

Invisibly cast on the calculated number of sts and work in st-st until the piece measures 5 cm less than the required overall length, ending with a wrong-side row.

Next calculate the width of the neck. This is usually approximately one-third of the shoulder measurement. Subtract this number of sts from the number of sts on the needle and divide the remainder by 2. This will give you the number of sts on each shoulder.

The next step is to shape the shoulders. (This step may be omitted if a straight shoulder is desired.) Knit the calculated number of shoulder sts on the right side, PM, knit the neck sts, PM, then knit one-third of the left shoulder sts and turn (see Special Techniques, page 11). Purl back across the left shoulder and neck sts, purl one-third of the right shoulder sts and turn. Knit back to left shoulder, knit two-thirds of the sts and turn. Continue in this manner until all the sts have been knitted up.

Front

Knit across the right shoulder sts, leave the neck sts on a stitch-holder, join in another ball of yarn and knit one-third of the left shoulder sts. Complete the front shoulder shapings as for the back.

Work the two sides of the front at the same time.

Round neck with front opening Continue without shaping for 5 cm, then begin the neck shaping. Divide the number of neck sts by 4. The result will give you the number of times to increase at the neck edges in alternate rows. When the increases are completed, calculate the number of sts to cast on. Divide the neck sts by 2, subtract 3, then divide the result by 2 (for example: 42 sts in neck, divide by 2 = 21, minus 3 = 18, divide by 2 = 9). Invisibly cast on this number of sts at neck edge in next two rows.

Continue without shaping until the front opening is the desired length. On the next row, work across one side, cast on 6 sts and work on to the other side.

V-neck Begin the neck shaping when the shoulder shaping has been completed. Increase at neck edges every 4th row on each side until you have added half the number of neck sts on each side. Work 3 more rows then join the two sides together.

Continue working without shaping until the front measures the same as the back. Thread remaining sts onto a length of left-over yarn.

Side panels

The next step is to calculate the number of rows which will be needed in the side panels. First take the chest measurement and subtract from it twice the shoulder measurement. Convert the result into rows and divide by 4. For example: Chest measurement, 100 cm; shoulder measurement, 37 cm; tension, 30 rows to 10 cm (or 3 rows to 1 cm). Subtract 2 × 37 (74) from 100 = 26 cm. Multiply this by 3 to convert into rows = 78. Divide this by 4 = 19.5, which can be rounded off to 20.

When you have calculated the number of rows for the side panels, with right side of work facing pick up sts along the left side of the central panel, taking two sts for every three rows. Work the calculated number of rows, dividing it into stripes of different colour and texture according to your preference.

When the calculated number of rows has been worked, the sts as far as the underarm are then joined together, either by grafting or by working them together according to one of the methods given in Special Techniques for joining shoulders. Calculate the number of sts needed for the sleeve and add 20. Subtract this number from the number of sts on the needle and divide the result by two. Mark this position on the needle and join the front and back sts to that point, either by grafting or by using one of the methods given for joining shoulders in Special Techniques on page 12).

Sleeves

When the side sts have been joined, divide the remaining sts on to 3 double-pointed needles and work the sleeve. Decrease at each end of every alternate round 10 times, then decrease every 4th or 6th round until the sleeve is 5 cm less than the desired length.

To work out the appropriate decrease intervals so that the sleeve will be the correct length, first calculate the number of rows in the shaped part of the sleeve (sleeve length minus 10 cm). Subtract the wrist sts from the upper arm sts and divide the result by 2. This will give you the number of decreasing rows. Divide the calculated number of rows in the shaped part of the sleeve first by 4 and then by 6. Choose whichever result is closest to the number of wrist sts but not less than that number. On the last round, decrease any excess sts evenly over the round so that the final number is equal to the number of sts required for the wrist.

Change to smaller-sized needles and work 5 cm in rib. Cast off loosely in rib.

Basque

With smaller sized circular needle and right side of work facing, knit up sts from invisible casting-on of back, then pick up sts along edge of side panel (see below). Knit sts threaded on left-over yarn on front, then pick up sts along edge of second side panel.

To calculate the number of sts to pick up along side panel, first calculate from your tension sample the number of sts which would be required for the chest measurement. Subtract the number of sts in the front and back panels then divide the result by two.

Work 5 cm in rib. Cast off loosely in rib.

Neckband for round neck

With smaller-sized needle, knit up sts from invisible casting on, then pick up 3 sts for every 4 rows up shaped side of neck. Knit sts from stitch-holder, then pick up 3 sts for every 4 rows down other side of neck and knit up sts from invisible casting on. Work 8 rows in rib. Cast off loosely in rib.

Front bands for round neck

Beginning at top edge of neckband, pick up one st for each row down side of left front opening and work 8 rows in rib. Cast off loosely in rib.

Work right band to correspond, making button-holes at regular intervals.

Neckband for V-neck

With smaller-sized double-pointed needles, knit up neck sts from stitch-holder, then knit up 3 sts for every 4 rows down left side. If you are going to work the band in K 1, P 1 rib, place a marker at this point then pick up 1 st from the centre of the V. If you are going to work the band in K 2, P 2 rib, first make sure that the number of sts is divisible by 4, then place a marker before the last 2 sts picked up on the side (centre of V). To ensure that these 2 centre sts are knit sts, it may be necessary to begin the rounds with P 2 instead of K 2. Knit up the same number of sts on the right side and divide the sts on to 3 needles. Work in rib until the band is the desired width, decreasing before and after the marker in every round if working in K 1, P 1 rib. If working in K 2, P 2 rib, work the decreases before the marker, then K 2 and decrease again. Cast off loosely in rib.

Making up

Darn in loose ends. For round-neck sweater stitch down ends of front bands to casting on and sew on buttons. Press if desired.

Multi-striped Dolman Sweater

Illustrated on page 25

This sweater is worked from the bottom up, and the sleeves are worked in one with the body. It features an attractive design of stripes in two contrasting colours. The neck is round with a deep collar in K 2, P 2 rib.

Fits chest size (cm)

A	B	C	D	E	F	G
80	85	**90**	95	**100**	105	**110**

Measures (cm)

90	95	**100**	105	**110**	115	**120**

Sleeve length, underarm to wrist (cm)

42	44	**45**	47	**48**	49	**50**

Materials

50 gm balls of 8-ply yarn
Main colour (M): **10**: 11: **11**: 12: **13**: 14: **15** balls
Contrasting colours (C1 and C2): 2 balls each.
80 cm circular needles and sets of four double-pointed needles in sizes 4 mm and 3.25 mm
2 stitch-holders

Tension

22 sts and 30 rows to 10 cm, measured over stocking stitch, using 4 mm needles.

INSTRUCTIONS

The work begins at the lower edge. Using 3.25 mm circular needle and M, cast on **200**: 212: **220**: 232: **244**: 256: **264** sts by the thumb method (see Special Techniques, page 11). Before proceeding any further make certain that there is no twist in the casting on. Place a marker to indicate the beginning of the round.

Work 5 cm in K 2, P 2 rib. In the first round, place a marker at the half-way point (**100**: 106: **110**: 116: **122**: 128: **132** sts).

Change to 4 mm circular needle and work **36**: 37: **38**: 40: **40**: 41: **42** cm in st-st.

Continue working without shaping, working stripes as follows:
1st and 2nd rounds: C1.
3rd round: M.
4th to 6th rounds: C1.
7th to 10th rounds: M.
11th round: C2.
12th round: M.
13th round: C1.
14th to 16th rounds: C2.
17th to 19th rounds: M.
20th round: C2.
21st round: C1.
22nd round: M.
23rd to 26th rounds: C1.
27th round: C2.
28th to 35th rounds: M.
36th round: C2.
37th round: M.
38th round: C1.
39th to 42nd rounds: C2.
43rd round: Still using C2, *K 1, inc 1, K to 1 st before marker, inc 1, K 1, SM*, rep from * to *.
44th round: K.

Rep 43rd and 44th rounds once.
47th round: Using M, K 1; using C1, inc 1; then K 1 in M, K 1 in C1 to 1 st before marker. Keeping sequence of colours correct, inc 1, K 1, SM, K 1, inc 1, work to last st, inc 1, K 1.

48th round: Work without shaping, working colours A and B as in previous round.

49th round: Increase as in 47th round, working M sts in C1 and C1 sts in M.

50th round: Work as 49th round, omitting increases.

51st round: Increase as in 47th round, working M sts in M and C1 sts in C1.

52nd round: Using C2, work without shaping.

53rd round: As 43rd round.

  Rep 52nd and 53rd round once.

56th round: Using M, work without shaping.

57th round: Still using M, work as 43rd round (**232**: 244: 252: 264: **276**: 288: **296** sts).

Back and sleeves

Still using M, invisibly cast on **81**: 86: **88**: 92: **95**: 97: **99** sts. Knit back across these sts, then K to marker and invisibly cast on **81**: 86: **88**: 92: **95**: 97: **99** sts (**278**: 294: **302**: 316: **328**: 338: **346** sts). Thread remaining sts onto a length of left-over yarn.

  Using M, work **1**: 1: **3**: 3: **3**: 5: **5** rows in st-st, then work striped pattern as follows:

1st row: C1.

2nd row: C2.

3rd row: M.

4th to 6th rows: C1.

7th and 8th rows: *Work 2 sts in C2, 1 st in C1*, rep to end.

9th row: Work C2 sts in C1 and C1 sts in C2.

10th row: Work C1 sts in C1 and C2 sts in C2.

11th to 13th rows: C2.

14th row: M.

15th row: C1.

16th row: M.

17th row: C2.

18th row: M.

19th row: C1.

20th to 23rd rows: M.

24th row: *M, 3 sts; C1, 1 st; C2, 1 st* rep from *to *to end of row.

25th to 28th rows: M.

29th row: C2.

30th row: C1.

  Using M, work **0**: 1: **1**: 1: **3**: 1: **3** rows.

Shape sleeves

1st and 2nd rows: Using C1, work to last **7**: 7: **6**: 7: **7**: 6: **6** sts, turn (see Special Techniques, page 11).

3rd row: Working alternate sts in C1 and C2, work to last **14**: 14: **12**: 14: **14**: 12: **12** sts, turn.

4th row: Using C2, work to last **14**: 14: **12**: 14: **14**: 12: **12** sts, turn.

5th and 6th rows: Still using C2, work to last **21**: 21: **18**: 21: **21**: 15: **18** sts, turn.

Complete the back and sleeves in M.

7th and 8th rows: Work to last **28**: 28: **24**: 28: **28**: 24: **24** sts, turn.

9th and 10th rows: Work to last **35**: 35: **30**: 35: **35**: 30: **30** sts, turn.

11th and 12th rows: Work to last **42**: 42: **36**: 42: **42**: 36: **36** sts, turn.

13th and 14th rows: Work to last **49**: 49: **42**: 49: **49**: 42: **42** sts, turn.

15th and 16th rows: Work to last **56**: 56: **48**: 56: **56**: 48: **48** sts, turn.

17th and 18th rows: Work to last **63**: 63: **54**: 63: **63**: 54: **54** sts, turn.

19th and 20th rows: Work to last **70**: 70: **60**: 70: **70**: 60: **60** sts, turn.

21st and 22nd rows: Work to last **77**: 77: **66**: 77: **77**: 66: **66** sts, turn.

Sizes C, D, E, F and G only: *23rd and 24th rows:* Work to last **72**: 84: **84**: 72: **72** sts, turn.

Sizes C, E, F and G only: *25th and 26th rows:* Work to last **78**: 91: 78: **78** sts, turn.

Sizes F and G only: *27th and 28th rows:* Work to last 84: **84** sts, turn.

Size G only: *29th and 30th rows:* Work to last 90 sts, turn.

Size G only: *31st and 32nd rows:* Work to last 96 sts, turn.

Shape shoulders

1st and 2nd rows: Work to last **81**: 86: **88**: 92: **95**: 97: **99** sts, PM, work **4**: 9: **10**: 8: **4**: 13: **3**, turn.

3rd and 4th rows: Work to **8**: 9: **9**: 9: **9**: 9: **10** sts before marker, turn.

5th and 6th rows: Work to **16**: 18: **18**: 18: **18**: 18: **20** sts before marker, turn.

7th and 8th rows: Work to **25**: 26: **26**: 27: **28**: 28: **29** sts before marker, turn.

9th row: Work **26**: 26: **28**: 28: **28**: 30: **30**, place these sts onto a stitch-holder, work to end.

  Thread remaining sts onto a length of left-over yarn.

Front and sleeves

Replace front sts on 4mm circular needle. Join in M, with right side facing, knit up **81**: 86: **88**: 92: **95**: 97: **99** sts from right sleeve invisible casting on. Purl back to left sleeve, pick up **81**: 86: **88**: 92: **95**: 97: **99** sts from invisible casting on.

  Work the front in the colour pattern to correspond with back. Work **30**: 32: **32**: 34: **36**: 36: **36** rows without shaping.

  When starting the sleeve shaping as for back, divide for neck as follows:

Next row: Work **125**: 132: **135**: 141: **146**: 150: **153** sts, place next **14**: 16: **16**: 18: **18**: 20: **20** sts on a stitch-holder.

Shape neck

The two sides of the front may now be worked separately, or a second ball of yarn joined in and the two sides worked at the same time.

Work 1 row. While continuing the sleeve shaping as for back, decrease 1 st at neck edge every alternate row **6**: 6: **7**: 7: **7**: 7: **7** times. Complete sleeve shaping as for back while working neck edge without shaping, then work shoulder shaping as for back.

Join sleeves and shoulders

Join the sleeve and shoulder sts together by one of the methods described in the Joining Shoulders section of Special Techniques, page 12.

Neckband

When the shoulders and sleeves are joined, using the same yarn, with right side of work facing, using set of four 3.25 mm double-pointed needles, join in yarn at back neck and knit up **26**: 26: **28**: 28: **28**: 30: **30** sts from stitch-holder. Knit up **20**: 20: **23**: 23: **23**: 23: **23** sts evenly down left front, knit up **14**: 14: **14**: 14: **14**: 16: **16** sts from stitch-holder, then **20**: 20: **23**: 23: **23**: 23: **23** sts evenly up right front (**80**: 80: **88**: 88: **88**: 92: **92** sts).

Work 7 cm in K 2, P 2 rib. Cast off loosely in rib.

Cuffs

With right side of work facing and using a set of four 3.25 mm double-pointed needles, knit up **44**: 44: **48**: 48: **52**: 52: **56** sts evenly around end of sleeve. Distribute sts evenly on to three needles.

Work 5 cm in K 2, P 2 rib. Cast off loosely in rib.

Making up

Darn in loose ends. Press if desired.

Dolman Sweater with Squared Pattern

Illustrated on page 45

This sweater is also worked from the bottom up, and the sleeves are worked in one with the body. It features a pattern of contrasting squares in three colours.

Fits chest size (cm)

A	B	C	D
85	95	**100**	110

Measures (cm)

92.5	101	**110**	118

Sleeve length, underarm to wrist (cm)

44	47	**48**	50

Materials

50 gm balls of 8-ply yarn
Main colour (M): 11: 12: 13: 14 balls
Contrasting colours (C1, C2 and C3): 1 ball each.
80 cm circular needles and sets of four double-pointed needles in sizes 5 mm and 4 mm
2 stitch-holders

Tension

19 sts and 26 rows to 10 cm, measured over stocking stitch, using 5 mm needles.

INSTRUCTIONS

The work begins at the lower edge. Using 4 mm circular needle and M, cast on **176**: 192: **208**: 224 sts by the thumb method (see page 11). Before proceeding any further make certain that there is no twist in the casting on. Place a marker to indicate the beginning of the round.

Work 5 cm in K 2, P 2 rib. In the first round, place a marker at the half-way point (**88**: 96: **104**: 112 sts).

Change to 5 mm circular needle and work 2 rounds in st-st.

In the next round, commence the squared pattern. The graph shows the placement of the contrasting squares. Each square on the graph represents **11**: 12: **13**: 14 sts and **15**: 16: **18**: 19 rounds. Use one of the methods given for Multi-coloured or Picture Knitting in the Round on page 13. Work without shaping until you have completed the 5th row of squares.
Next round: *K 1, inc 1, K to 1 st before marker, inc 1, K 1, SM*, rep from * to *.
Next round: K.

Rep these 2 rounds 7 times (**208**: 224: **240**: 256 sts).

Back and sleeves

Invisibly cast on **74**: 80: **82**: 86 sts, placing a marker before the cast-on sts. Knit back across these sts, then K to marker, SM and invisibly cast on **74**: 80: **82**: 86 sts (**252**: 272: **284**: 300 sts). Thread remaining sts on to a length of left-over yarn.

Keeping continuity of squared pattern, work sleeve shaping as follows:
1st and 2nd rows: Work to marker, work **7**: 8: **6**: 6 sts, turn (see page 11).
3rd and 4th rows: Work to marker, work **14**: 16: **12**: 12 sts, turn.
5th and 6th rows: Work to marker, work **21**: 24: **18**: 18 sts, turn.

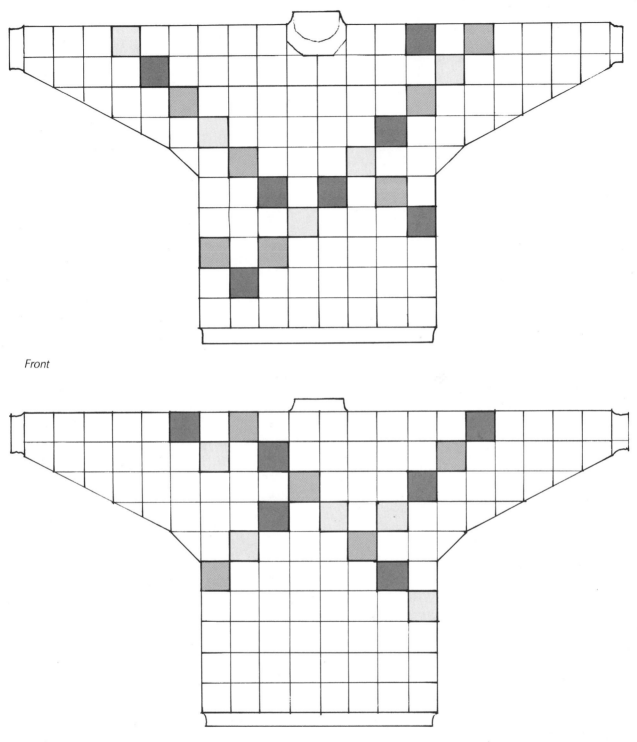

Front

Back

7th and 8th rows: Work to marker, work **28**: **32**: **24**: 24 sts, turn.

9th and 10th rows: Work to marker, work **35**: **40**: **30**: 30 sts, turn.

11th and 12th rows: Work to marker, work **42**: **48**: **36**: 36 sts, turn.

13th and 14th rows: Work to marker, work **49**: **56**: **42**: 42 sts, turn.

15th and 16th rows: Work to marker, work **56**: **64**: **48**: 48 sts, turn.

17th and 18th rows: Work to marker, work **63**: **72**: **54**: 54 sts, turn.

19th and 20th rows: Work to marker, work **74**: **80**: **60**: 60 sts, turn.

Sizes C and D only:

21st and 22nd rows: Work to marker, work 66 sts, turn.
23rd and 24th rows: Work to marker, work 72 sts, turn.
25th and 26th rows: Work to marker, work 82: 78 sts, turn.

Size D only:

27th and 28th rows: Work to marker, work 86 sts, turn.
All sizes: Keeping continuity of squared pattern, work another **27**: 29: **29**: 31 rows without shaping.

Thread first **115**: 124: **130**: 137 sts onto a length of left-over yarn, place **22**: 24: **24**: 26 sts on a stitch-holder, then thread the rest of the sts onto a length of left-over yarn.

Front and sleeves

Replace front sts on 5 mm circular needle. With right side facing, knit up **74**: 80: **82**: 86 sts from invisible casting on. Purl back to left sleeve, knit up **74**: 80: **82**: 86 sts from invisible casting on.

Work sleeve shaping as for back, then work 4: 4: 4: 6 rows without shaping.

Divide for neck as follows:
Next row: Knit **175**: 124: **130**: 137, place next **12**: 12: **12**: 14 sts on a stitch holder.

Shape neck

The two sides of the front may now be worked separately, or a second ball of yarn joined in and the two sides worked at the same time.

Work 1 row, then decrease 1 st at neck edge every alternate row **5**: 6: **6**: 6 times.
Work 14 rows without shaping.

Join sleeves and shoulders

Join the sleeve and shoulder sts together by one of the methods described in the Joining Shoulders section on page 12.

Neckband

When the shoulders and sleeves are joined, using the same yarn, with right side of work facing, using set of four 4 mm double-pointed needles, join in yarn at back neck and knit up **22**: 24: **24**: 26 sts from stitch-holder. Pick up **17**: 18: **18**: 18 sts evenly down left front, knit up **12**: 12: **12**: 14 sts from stitch-holder, then **17**: 18: **18**: 18 sts evenly up right front (**68**: 72: **72**: 76 sts).

Work 12 rows in K 2, P 2 rib. Cast off loosely in rib.

Cuffs

With right side of work facing and using a set of four 4 mm double-pointed needles, knit up **40**: 40: **44**: 44 sts evenly around end of sleeve. Distribute sts evenly on to 3 needles.

Work 5 cm in K 2, P 2 rib. Cast off loosely in rib.

Making up

Darn in loose ends. Press if desired.

Dolman Sweater

First make a tension sample (see page 10) and take measurements (see page 11).

Body

From the chest measurement, calculate the number of sts required. Using a circular needle two sizes smaller than that to be used for the main part of the work, cast on this number of sts by the thumb method (see page 11). Before going any further check that there is no twist in the casting on. Place a marker at the beginning of the round and at the half-way point. Work 5 cm in rib. If using K 2, P 2 rib, make sure that the number of sts is divisible by 4.

Change to larger sized needles and work until body is required length to underarm, working contrasting stripes in your own design. Work stripes in a combination of single colours and two colours, or even in simple geometrical shapes (checking first that the shape fits with the number of sts in the round).

Before beginning the sleeves, inc 1 st at the beginning of the round, before and after the half-way marker and at the end of the round. Work 1 row without shaping. Repeat these two rounds 7 times.

Back and sleeves

Calculate the number of sts to correspond with the length of the sleeve, minus 5 cm, and invisibly cast on this number (see page 11). Work across cast-on sts and across half the body sts (back), then invisibly cast on the same number of sleeve sts. Thread front sts onto a length of left-over yarn. Work in rows without shaping until the sleeve measures half the wrist measurement.

Calculate the number of sts to correspond with the shoulder measurement. Locate this number of sts in the centre of the row and place a marker at each end.

Using the row tension, calculate the number of rows required for the upper arm measurement. Subtract from that number the number of rows already worked in the sleeve. The shaping of the top of the sleeve is now worked in steps. To obtain the number of steps, subtract the number of rows in half the wrist from the number of rows in half the upper arm and divide the result by 2. The number of sts in each step will then be the number of sleeve sts divided by the number of steps. Work these steps as short rows, working to the calculated number of sts in each step from the end of the sleeve, turning (see page 11) and working to the same point on the other sleeve. Continue working the steps in this manner until the sleeve is completed.

The sleeve shaping may be done on the underside of the sleeve, after the invisible casting on. Work the short rows in the same way, then work the required number of rows for half the wrist.

The next step is to shape the shoulders. (This step may be omitted if a straight shoulder is desired.) First calculate the neck sts by dividing the shoulder sts by three. Locate these sts at the centre of the row and place a marker at each end. There is now a marker at each end of each shoulder. Divide the number of sts in each shoulder side by 3 and work the shoulder shapings in 3 steps of short rows, as for sleeve shapings. Place the neck sts on a stitch-holder and thread the sleeve sts on to a length of left-over yarn.

Front and sleeves

Replace front sts on circular needle. Knit up right sleeve sts from invisible casting on, work across front sts, then knit up left sleeve sts from invisible casting on. Work as for back and sleeves until you reach the desired depth of the neck opening. Subtract the number of neck sts previously calculated from the total number of sts on the needle and divide this number by 2. Work that number of sts, then complete the left side of the front on these sts. Decrease in alternate rows until you have taken out one-quarter of the neck sts, then complete the left side to correspond with the back. Place one half of the neck sts on a stitch-holder, then complete the right side to correspond with the left.

Join the sleeve and shoulder sts together by one of the methods described in Joining Shoulders on page 12.

Neckband

When the shoulders and sleeves are joined, using the same yarn, with right side of work facing, using smaller sized double-pointed needles, knit up sts from back stitch-holder. Pick up 3 sts for 4 rows down left side of front, then knit the sts from the front stitch-holder. Pick up 3 sts for 4 rows up right side of front. Work in rib until band is desired width. If using K 2, P 2 rib, make sure that the number of sts is divisible by 4.

Cuffs

Calculate the number of sts to correspond with the wrist measurement. Using double-pointed needles two sizes smaller, knit up this number of sts from end of sleeve and distribute them evenly onto 3 needles. Work 5 cm in rib. If you are using K 2, P 2 rib, be sure that the number of sts is divisible by 4.

Making up

Darn in loose ends. Press if desired.

Multi-striped dolman sweater
(page 27)

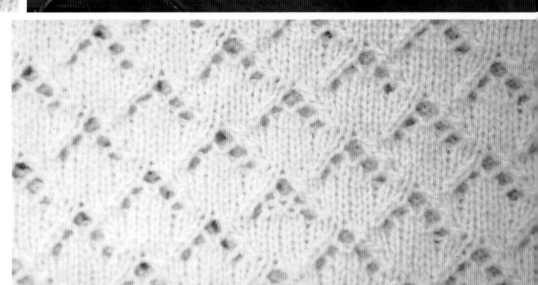

Lightweight lacy sweater (facing page), with details of the allover lace pattern in the body and the chain pattern in the sleeves

Lacy Sweater

Illustrated on facing page

This light attractive sweater features a simple all-over lace pattern in the body and a lacy chain pattern in the shoulder saddle and sleeve.

Fits chest size (cm)

A	B	C	D	E	F	G
80	85	**90**	95	**100**	105	**110**

Measures (cm)

88.5	92	**100**	104	**111**	115	**119**

Sleeve length, underarm to wrist (cm)

42	44	**45**	47	**48**	49	**50**

Materials

50 gm balls of 5-ply yarn
10: 10: **11**: 11: **12**: 13: **13** balls
80 cm circular needles and sets of four double-pointed needles in sizes 3.75 mm and 3 mm
Small quantity of left-over yarn
3 stitch-holders

Tension

26 sts and 36 rows to 10 cm, measured over stocking stitch, using 3.75 mm needles.

INSTRUCTIONS

The first step is to work the two shoulder saddles. Using 3.75 mm needles, invisibly cast on **17**: 16: **16**: 23: **25**: 24: **25** sts.
1st row: (right side) K **6**: 5: **8**: 9: **10**: 9: **10**, yfwd, sl 1, K 1, psso, K 2, yfwd, sl 1, K 1, psso, K **5**: 5: **8**: 8: **9**: 9: **9**.
2nd and alternate (even-numbered) *rows:* P.
3rd row: K **4**: 3: **6**: 7: **8**: 7: **8**, k 2 tog, yfwd, K 1, yfwd, sl 1, K 1, psso, K 2, yfwd, sl 1, K 1, psso, K **4**: 4: **7**: 7: **8**: 8: **8**.
5th row: K **3**: 2: **5**: 6: **7**: 6: **7**, K 2 tog, yfwd, K 3, yfwd, sl 1, K 1, psso, K 2, yfwd, sl 1, K 1, psso, K **3**: 3: **6**: 6: **7**: 7: **7**.
7th row: K **2**: 1: **4**: 5: **6**: 5: **6**, K 2 tog, yfwd, K 2, K 2 tog, yfwd, K 1, yfwd, sl 1, K 1, psso, K 2, yfwd, sl 1, K 1, psso, K **2**: 2: **5**: 5: **6**: 6: **6**.
9th row: K **1**: 0: **3**: 4: **5**: 4: **5**, K 2 tog, yfwd, K 2, K 2 tog, yfwd, K 3, yfwd, sl 1, K 1, psso, K 2, yfwd, sl 1, K 1, psso, K **1**: 1: **4**: 4: **5**: 5: **5**.
11th row: K **3**: 2: **5**: 6: **7**: 6: **7**, yfwd, sl 1, K 1, psso, K 2, yfwd, sl 1, K 1, psso, yfwd, K 2 tog, yfwd, K 2, K 2 tog, yfwd, K 2 tog, K **0**: 0: **3**: 3: **4**: 4: **4**.
13th row: K **4**: 3: **6**: 7: **8**: 7: **8**, yfwd, sl 1, K 1, psso, K 2, yfwd, sl 1, K 2 tog, psso, yfwd, K 2, K 2 tog, yfwd, K **2**: 2: **5**: 5: **6**: 6: **6**.
15th row: K **5**: 4: **7**: 8: **9**: 8: **9**, yfwd, sl 1, K 1, psso, K 2, yfwd, sl 1, K 1, psso, K 1, K 2 tog, yfwd, K **3**: 3: **6**: 6: **7**: 7: **7**.
16th row: P.

These 16 rows complete the pattern. Work another **30**: 30: **34**: 36: **38**: 38: **38** rows in pattern. Break off yarn and leave sts on a stitch-holder. Work another saddle to correspond.

Now begin the back. Using 3.75 mm circular needle, with right side of work facing, pick up **30**: 30: **33**: 34: **35**: 36: **35** sts evenly along long side of one shoulder saddle, starting at stitch-holder end.

Invisibly cast on **26**: 28: **28**: 28: **30**: 30: **32** sts, then pick up **30**: 30: **33**: 34: **35**: 36: **35** sts evenly along long side of second shoulder saddle, starting at cast-on end (**86**: 88: **94**: 96: **100**: 102: **102** sts).
1st row: P.
2nd row: K **66**: 68: **72**: 74: **76**: 78: **78**, turn (see page 11).

3rd row: P **46**: 48: **50**: 52: **52**: 54: **54**, turn.
4th row: K **56**: 58: **61**: 63: **64**: 66: **66**, turn.
5th row: P **66**: 68: **72**: 74: **76**: 78: **78**, turn.
6th row: K to end.
7th row: P.
 Break off yarn, leave sts on circular needle.

Front shoulders

Join in yarn at stitch-holder end of right shoulder saddle. Using the same circular needle, with right side of work facing, pick up **30**: 30: **33**: 34: **35**: 36: **35** sts evenly along side. Using a second ball of yarn, join in yarn to cast-on end of left shoulder saddle and pick up **30**: 30: **33**: 34: **35**: 36: **35** sts evenly along side.

1st row: P across left and right fronts.
2nd row: K back across right front, K **10**: 10: **11**: 12: **11**: 12: **11** on left front, turn.
3rd row: P back across left front, P **10**: 10: **11**: 12: **11**: 12: **11** on right front, turn.
4th row: K back across right front, K **20**: 20: **22**: 22: **24**: 24: **24** on left front, turn.
5th row: P back across left front, P **20**: 20: **22**: 22: **24**: 24: **24** on right front, turn.
6th row: K back across right front, K to end of left front.
7th row: P across left front, P to end of right front.
 Break off yarn from right front and slip the right-front sts on to the right-hand end of the circular needle.

Sleeve top and neck shaping

1st row: **Size A**: K 7, *yfwd, sl 1, K 1, psso, K 8*, rep from * to * once, yfwd, sl 1, K 1, psso, K 1; **size B**: K 6, rep from * to * (as in size A) twice, yfwd, sl 1, K 1, psso, K 2; **size C**: K 6, rep from * to * (as in size A) twice, yfwd, sl 1, K 1, psso, K 5; **size D**: K 6, rep from * to * (as in size A) twice, yfwd, sl 1, K 1, psso, K 6; **size E**: K 5, rep from * to * (as in size A) 3 times; **size F**: K 5, rep from * to * (as in size A) 3 times, K 1; **size G**: K 4, rep from * to * (as in size A) 3 times, K 1; **all sizes**: **PM, knit up 1 st from side edge, work sts from stitch-holder in pattern, knit up 1 st from edge of back, PM**; **size A**: K 8, rep from * to * 7 times, yfwd, sl 1, K 1, psso, K 6; **size B**: K 4, rep from * to * 8 times, yfwd, sl 1, K 1, psso, K 2; **size C**: K 7, rep from * to * 8 times, yfwd, sl 1, K 1, psso, K 5; **size D**: K 3, rep from * to * 9 times, yfwd, sl 1, K 1, psso, K 1; **size E**: K 5, rep from * to * 9 times, yfwd, sl 1, K 1, psso, K 3; **size F**: K 1, rep from * to * 10 times, K 1; **size G**: K 6, rep from * to * 9 times, yfwd, sl 1, K 1, psso, K 4; **all sizes**: rep from ** to **; **size A**: K 3, rep from * to * twice, yfwd, sl 1, K 1, psso, K 5; **size B**: K 4, rep from * to * twice, yfwd, sl 1, K 1, psso, K 4; **size C**: K 7, rep from * to * twice, yfwd, sl 1, K 1, psso, K 4; **size D**: K 8, rep from * to * twice, yfwd, sl 1, K 1, psso, K 4; **size E**: rep from * to * 3 times, yfwd, sl 1, K 1, psso, K 3; **size F**: K 1, rep from * to * 3 times, yfwd, sl 1, K 1, psso, K 3; **size G**: K 1, rep from * to * 3 times, yfwd, sl 1, K 1, psso, K 2.

2nd row: *P to marker, SM, inc 1 P, P **19**: 18: **24**: 25: **27**: 26: **27**, inc 1 P, SM, rep from * to *, P to end.
3rd row: **Size A**: K 1, inc 1, K 4, K 2 tog, yfwd, *K 1, yfwd, sl 1, K 1, psso, K 5, K 2 tog, yfwd*; rep from * to *, K 3; **size B**: K 1, inc 1, K 3, K 2 tog, yfwd, rep from * to * (as in size A) twice, K 1, yfwd, sl 1, K 1, psso, K 1; **size C**: K 1, inc 1, K 3, K 2 tog, yfwd, rep from * to * (as in size A) twice, K 1, yfwd, sl 1, K 1, psso, K 4; **size D**: K 1, inc 1, K 3, K 2 tog, yfwd, rep from * to * (as in size A) twice, K 1, yfwd, sl 1, K 1, psso, K 5; **size E**: K 1, inc 1, K 2, K 2 tog, yfwd, rep from * to * (as in size A) 3 times; **size F**: K 1, inc 1, K 2, K 2 tog, yfwd, rep from * to * (as in size A) 3 times, K 1; **size G**: K 1, inc 1, K 1, K 2 tog, yfwd, rep from * to * (as in size A) 3 times, K 1; **all sizes**: **SM, inc 1, work **21**: 20: **26**: 27: **29**: 28: **29** in pattern, inc 1, SM**; **size A**: K 6, K 2 tog, yfwd, rep from * to * 7 times, K 1, yfwd, sl 1, K 1, psso, K 5; **size B**: K 2, K 2 tog, yfwd, rep from * to * 8 times, K 1 yfwd, sl 1, K 1, psso, K 1; **size C**: K 5, K 2 tog, yfwd, rep from * to * 8 times, K 1, yfwd, sl 1, K 1, psso, K 4; **size D**: K 1, K 2 tog, yfwd, rep from * to * 9 times, K 3; **size E**: K 3, K 2 tog, yfwd, rep from * to * 9 times, K 1, yfwd, sl 1, K 1, psso, K 2; **size F**: K 1, rep from * to * 10 times, K 1; **size G**: K 4, K 2 tog, yfwd, rep from * to * 9 times, K 1, yfwd, sl 1, K 1, psso, K 3; **all sizes**: rep from ** to **; **size A**: K 1, K 2 tog, yfwd, rep from * to * twice, K 1, yfwd, sl 1, K 1, psso, K 3, inc 1, K 1; **size B**: K 2, K 2 tog, yfwd, K 1, rep from * to * twice, K 1, yfwd, sl 1, K 1, psso, K 2, inc 1, K 1; **size C**: K 5, K 2 tog, yfwd, rep from * to * twice, K 1, yfwd, sl 1, K 1, psso, K 2, inc 1, K 1; **size D**: K 6, K 2 tog, yfwd, rep from * to * twice, K 1, yfwd, sl 1, K 1, psso, K 2, inc 1, K 1; **size E**: rep from * to * 3 times, K 1, yfwd, sl 1, K 1, psso, K 1, inc 1, K 1; **size F**: K 1, rep from * to * 3 times, K 1, yfwd, sl 1, K 1, psso, K 1, inc 1, K 1; **size G**: K 1, rep from * to * 3 times, K 1, yfwd, sl 1, K 1, psso, inc 1, K 1.

4th row: *P to marker, SM, inc 1 P, P **23**: 22: **28**: 29: **31**: 30: **31**, inc 1 P, SM*, rep from * to *, P to end.
5th row: **Size A**: K 5, K 2 tog, yfwd, K 1, *K 2, yfwd, sl 1, K 1, psso, K 3, K 2 tog, yfwd, K 1*, rep from * to *, K 3; **size B**: K 4, K 2 tog, yfwd, K 1, rep from * to * (as in size A) twice, K 4; **size C**: K 4, K 2 tog, yfwd, K 1, rep from * to * (as in size A) twice, K 2, yfwd, sl 1, K 1, psso, K 3; **size D**: K 4, K 2 tog, yfwd, K 1, rep from * to * (as in size A) twice, K 2, yfwd, sl 1, K 1, psso, K 4; **size E**: K 3, K 2 tog, yfwd, K 1, rep from * to * (as in size A) 3 times; **size F**: K 3, K 2 tog, yfwd, K 1, rep from * to * (as in size A) 3 times, K 1; **size G**: K 2, K 2 tog, yfwd,

38

K 1, rep from * to * (as in size A) 3 times, K 1; **all sizes**: **SM, inc 1, work 25: 24: **30**: 31: **33**: 32: **33** in pattern, inc 1, SM**, **size A**: K 5, K 2 tog, yfwd, K 1, rep from * to * 7 times, K 2, yfwd, sl 1, K 1, psso, K 4; **size B**: K 1, K 2 tog, yfwd, K 1, rep from * to * 8 times, K 4; **size C**: K 4, K 2 tog, yfwd, K 1, rep from * to * 8 times, K 2, yfwd, sl 1, K 1, psso, K 3; **size D**: K 3, rep from * to * 9 times, K 3; **size E**: K 2, K 2 tog, yfwd, K 1, rep from * to * 9 times, K 2, yfwd, sl 1, K 1, psso, K 1; **size F**: K 1, rep from * to * 10 times, K 1; **size G**: K 3, K 2 tog, yfwd, K 1, rep from * to * 9 times, K 2, yfwd, sl 1, K 1, psso, K 2; **all sizes**: rep from ** to **; **size A**: K 3, rep from * to * twice; K 2, yfwd, sl 1, K 1, psso, K 4; **size B**: K 1, K 2 tog, yfwd, K 1, rep from * to * twice, K 2, yfwd, sl 1, K 1, psso, K 3; **size C**: K 4, K 2 tog, yfwd, K 1, rep from * to * twice, K 2, yfwd, sl 1, K 1, psso, K 3; **size D**: K 5, K 2 tog, yfwd, K 1, rep from * to * twice, K 2, yfwd, sl 1, K 1, psso, K 3; **size E**: rep from * to * 3 times, K 2, yfwd, sl 1, K 1, psso, K 2; **size F**: K 1, rep from * to * 3 times, K 2, yfwd, sl 1, K 1, psso, K 2; **size G**: K 1, rep from * to * 3 times, K 2, yfwd, sl 1, K 1, psso, K 1.

6th row: *P to marker, SM, inc 1 P, P 27: 26: **32**: 33: **35**: 34: **35**, inc 1 P, SM*, rep from * to *, P to end.

7th row: **Size A**: K 1, inc 1, K 2, yfwd, sl 1, K 1, psso, K 3, *K 5, yfwd, sl 1, K 1, psso, K 3*, rep from * to *, K 3; **size B**: K 1, inc 1, K 1, yfwd, sl 1, K 1, psso, K 3, rep from * to * (as in size A), twice, K 4; **size C**: K 1, inc 1, K 1, yfwd, sl 1, K 1, psso, K 3, rep from * to * (as in size A) twice, K 7; **size D**: K 1, inc 1, K 1, yfwd, sl 1, K 1, psso, K 3, rep from * to * (as in size A) twice, K 5, yfwd, sl 1, K 1, psso, K 1; **size E**: K 1, inc 1, yfwd, sl 1, K 1, psso, K 3, rep from * to * (as in size A) 3 times; **size F**: K 1, inc 1, yfwd, sl 1, K 1, psso, K 3, rep from * to * (as in size A) 3 times, K 1; **size G**: K 1, inc 1, K 4, rep from * to * (as in size A) 3 times, K 1; **all sizes**: **SM, inc 1, work 29: 28: **34**: 35: **37**: 36: **37** in pattern, inc 1, SM**, **size A**: K 3, yfwd, sl 1, K 1, psso, K 3, rep from * to * 7 times, K 5, yfwd, sl 1, K 1, psso, K 1; **size B**: K 4, rep from * to * 8 times, K 4; **size C**: K 2, yfwd, sl 1, K 1, psso, K 3, rep from * to * 8 times, K 7; **size D**: K 3, rep from * to * 9 times, K 3; **size E**: K 5, rep from * to * 9 times, K 5; **size F**: K 1, rep from * to * 10 times, K 1; **size G**: K 1, yfwd, sl 1, K 1, psso, K 3, rep from * to * 9 times, K 6; **all sizes**: rep from ** to **; **size A**: K 3, rep from * to * twice, K 5, yfwd, sl 1, K 1, psso, inc 1, K 1; **size B**: K 4, rep from * to * twice, K 6, inc 1, K 1; **size C**: K 2, yfwd, sl 1, K 1, psso, K 3, rep from * to * twice, K 1, yfwd, sl 1, K 1, psso, K 3, inc 1, K 1; **size D**: K 3, yfwd, sl 1, K 1, psso, K 3, rep from * to * twice, K 1, yfwd, sl 1, K 1, psso, K 3, inc 1, K 1; **size E**: rep from * to * 3 times, K 5, inc 1, K 1; **size F**: K 1, rep from * to * 3 times, K 5, inc 1, K 1; **size G**: K 1, rep from * to * 3 times, K 4, inc 1, K 1.

8th row: P.

9th row: **Size A**: K 2, K 2 tog, yfwd, K 1, yfwd, sl 1, K 1, psso, K 2, *K 3, K 2 tog, yfwd, K 1, yfwd, sl 1, K 1, psso, K 2*, rep from * to *, K 3; **size B**: K 1, K 2 tog, yfwd, K 1, yfwd, sl 1, K 1, psso, K 2, rep from * to * (as in size A) twice, K 4; **size C**: K 1, K 2 tog, yfwd, K 1, yfwd, sl 1, K 1, psso, K 2, rep from * to * (as in size A) twice, K 3, K 2 tog, yfwd, K 2; **size D**: K 1, K 2 tog, yfwd, K 1, yfwd, sl 1, K 1, psso, K 2, rep from * to * (as in size A) twice, K 3, K 2 tog, yfwd, K 3; **size E**: K 3, yfwd, sl 1, K 1, psso, K 2, rep from * to * (as in size A) 3 times; **size F**: K 3, yfwd, sl 1, K 1, psso, K 2, rep from * to * (as in size A) 3 times, K 1; **size G**: K 2, yfwd, sl 1, K 1, psso, K 2, rep from * to * 3 times, K 1; **all sizes**: **SM, inc 1, work in pattern to next marker, inc 1, SM**, **size A**: K 1, K 2 tog, yfwd, K 1, yfwd, sl 1, K 1, psso, K 2, rep from * to * 7 times, K 3, K 2 tog, yfwd, K 3; **size B**: K 4, rep from * to * 8 times, K 4; **size C**: K 3, yfwd, sl 1, K 1, psso, K 2, rep from * to * 8 times, K 3, K 2 tog, yfwd, K 2; **size D**: K 3, rep from * to * 9 times, K 3; **size E**: K 1, yfwd, sl 1, K 1, psso, K 2, rep from * to * 9 times, K 5; **size F**: K 1, rep from * to * 10 times, K 1; **size G**: K 2, yfwd, sl 1, K 1, psso, K 2, rep from * to * 9 times, K 3, K 2 tog, yfwd, K 1; **all sizes**: rep from ** to **; **size A**: K 3, rep from * to * twice, K 3, K 2 tog, yfwd, K 1, yfwd, sl 1, K 1, psso, K 1; **size B**: K 4, rep from * to * twice, K 3, K 2 tog, yfwd, K 3; **size C**: K 3, yfwd, sl 1, K 1, psso, K 2, rep from * to * twice, K 3, K 2 tog, yfwd, K 3; **size D**: K 1, K 2 tog, yfwd, K 1, yfwd, sl 1, K 1, psso, K 2, rep from * to * twice, K 3, K 2 tog, yfwd, K 3; **size E**: rep from * to * 3 times, K 3, K 2 tog, yfwd, K 2; **size F**: K 1, rep from * to * 3 times, K 3, K 2 tog, yfwd, K 2; **size G**: K 1, rep from * to * 3 times, K 3, K 2 tog, yfwd, K 1.

10th row: P.

11th row: **Size A**: K 1, inc 1, K 2 tog, yfwd, K 3, yfwd, sl 1, K 1, psso, K 1, *K 2, K 2 tog, yfwd, K 3, yfwd, sl 1, K 1, psso, K 1*, rep from * to *, K 3; **size B**: K 1, inc 1, K 4, yfwd, sl 1, K 1, psso, K 1, rep from * to * (as in size A) twice, K 4; **size C**: K 1, inc 1, K 4, yfwd, sl 1, K 1, psso, K 1, rep from * to * (as in size A) twice, K 2, K 2 tog, yfwd, K 3; **size D**: K 1, inc 1, K 4, yfwd, sl 1, K 1, psso, K 1, rep from * to * (as in size A) twice, K 2, K 2 tog, yfwd, K 4; **size E**: K 1, inc 1, K 3, yfwd, sl 1, K 1, psso, K 1, rep from * to * (as in size A) 3 times; **size F**: K 1, inc 1, K 3, yfwd, sl 1, K 1, psso, K 1, rep from * to * (as in size A) 3 times, K 1; **size G**: K 1, inc 1, K 2, yfwd, sl 1, K 1, psso, K 1, rep from * to * (as in size A) 3 times, K 1; **all sizes**: **SM, work in pattern to next marker, inc 1, SM**; **size A**: K 2 tog, yfwd, K 3, yfwd, sl 1, K 1, psso, K 1, rep from * to * 7 times, K 2, K 2 tog, yfwd, K 4; **size B**: K 1, yfwd, sl 1, K 1, psso, K 1, rep from * to * 8 times, K 4; **size C**: K 4, yfwd, sl 1, K 1, psso, K 1, rep from *

to * 8 times, K 2, K 2 tog, yfwd, K 3; **size D**: K 3, rep from * to * 9 times, K 3; **size E**: K 2, yfwd, sl 1, K 1, psso, K 1, rep from * to * 9 times, K 2, K 2 tog, yfwd, K 1; **size F**: K 1, rep from * to * 10 times, K 1; **size G**: K 3, yfwd, sl 1, K 1, psso, K 1, rep from * to * 9 times, K 2, K 2 tog, yfwd, K 2; **all sizes**: rep from ** to **; **size A**: K 3, rep from * to * twice, K 2, K 2 tog, yfwd, K 4, inc 1, K 1; **size B**: K 1, yfwd, sl 1, K 1, psso, K 1, rep from * to * twice, K 2, K 2 tog, yfwd, K 3, inc 1, K 1; **size C**: K 4, yfwd, sl 1, K 1, psso, K 1, rep from * to * twice, K 2, K 2 tog, yfwd, K 3, inc 1, K 1; **size D**: K 5, yfwd, sl 1, K 1, psso, K 1, rep from * to * twice, K 2, K 2 tog, yfwd, K 3, inc 1, K 1; **size E**: rep from * to * 3 times, K 2, K 2 tog, yfwd, K 2, inc 1, K 1; **size F**: K 1, rep from * to * 3 times, K 2, K 2 tog, yfwd, K 2, inc 1, K 1; **size G**: K 1, rep from * to * 3 times, K 2, K 2 tog, yfwd, K 1, inc 1, K 1.
12th row: P.

These 12 rows complete the lace pattern for the body. Continue in this manner, keeping body and sleeve patterns correct, increasing at armhole markers next and every alternate row and at neck edge every 4th row until there are **59**: 62: **66**: 65: **65**: 66: **65** sts in the sleeve caps (between markers).

To shape the body sections at underarms, increase in next row as follows: *Work to 1 st before marker, inc 1, K 1, SM, inc 1, work to next marker, inc 1, SM, K 1, inc 1*, work to end.

Continue in this manner, increasing at armhole edges as before. At the same time, increase as in previous row on fronts and back every alternate row **6**: 7: **8**: 9: **11**: 11: **13** more times, while also continuing to increase at neck edge every 4th row (**346**: 364: **392**: 402: **426**: 432: **446** sts).

Work 1 row (wrong side). Break off yarn and slip left front sts (to 1st marker) onto right-hand needle point.

Left sleeve

Change to 3.75 mm double-pointed needles and work sleeve sts to second marker, dividing sts onto 3 needles. Invisibly cast on **15: 16: **18**: 19: **21**: 24: **25** sts, placing half the cast-on sts on the 1st double-pointed needle and half on the 3rd (**88**: 94: **102**: 104: **110**: 114: **118** sts).**

Thread remaining sts on the circular needle onto a length of left-over yarn, taking care to keep the right sleeve markers in place.

Keeping continuity of pattern, work in rounds until the sleeve measures 5 cm. *Note:* Knit alternate rounds instead of purling them.
Next round: K 1, K 2 tog, work to last 3 sts, sl 1, K 1, psso, K 1.

Continue to decrease in this manner every 6th round until **48**: 52: **60**: 58: **64**: 66: **70** sts remain. Work 5 rounds without shaping.

Next round: Decrease **0**: 0: **4**: 2: **4**: 6: **6** sts evenly over round (**52**: 52: **56**: 56: **60**: 64: **64** sts).

Change to 3 mm double-pointed needles and work 5 cm in K 2, P 2 rib. Cast off loosely in rib.

Right sleeve

Using the circular needle, join in yarn at left-front end of underarm casting on. Work across cast-on sts. Keeping pattern correct, work the sts from the length of yarn across the back to the next marker. Repeat from ** to **.

Body

Using 3.75 mm circular needle, join in yarn at right-back end of underarm casting on. Work across approximately half the cast-on sts, PM (place this marker to correspond with the beginning of a pattern repeat), work the rest of the cast-on sts, then work the rest of the sts from the length of yarn (**230**: 240: **260**: 270: **290**: 300: **310** sts).

Continue working in rounds, keeping the marker in place and continuing the lace pattern across the underarm sts, until the body is the desired length minus 8 cm, ending with a 6th or 12th pattern round, decreasing **2**: 0: **0**: 2: **2**: 0: **2** sts evenly over last round (**228**: 240: **260**: 268: **288**: 300: **308** sts)

Beginning at the marker, change to 3 mm circular needle and work in K 2, P 2 rib for 8 cm. Cast off loosely in rib.

Neckband

Using 3 mm double-pointed needles, with right side of work facing, join in yarn at right-back end of invisibly cast-on sts and K **26**: 28: **28**: 28: **30**: 30: **32**. Knit up **17**: 16: **22**: 23: **25**: 24: **25** sts from shoulder saddle casting on, then **41**: 42: **42**: 43: **43**: 44: **45** sts evenly along left front, placing a marker before the last 2 sts. Knit up **39**: 42: **42**: 43: **41**: 42: **45** sts evenly along right front and **17**: 16: **22**: 23: **25**: 24: **25** sts from shoulder saddle casting on (**140**: 144: **156**: 160: **164**: 164: **172** sts). Divide sts on to 3 needles.
1st round: Sizes A and C: (P 2, K 2) to end. **Sizes B, D, E, F and G**: (K 2, P 2) to end.
2nd round: **Sizes A and C**: (P 2, K 2) to 2 sts before marker, P 2 tog, SM, K 2, P 2 tog, K 2, (P 2, K 2) to end, K 2. **Sizes B, D, E, F and G**: (K 2, P 2) to 4 sts before marker, K 2, P 2 tog, SM, K 2, P 2 tog, (K 2, P 2) to end.
3rd round: **Sizes A and C**: (P 2, K 2) to 5 sts before marker, P 2, K 1, sl 1, K 1, psso, SM, K 2, K 2 tog, K 1, (P 2, K 2) to end. **Sizes B, D, E, F and G**: (K 2, P 2) to 3 sts before marker, K 1, sl 1, K 1, psso, SM, K 2 tog, P 2, (K 2, P 2) to end.
4th round: **Sizes A and C**: (P 2, K 2) to 4 sts before

marker, P 2, sl 1, K 1, psso, SM, K 2, K 2 tog, (P 2, K 2) to end. **Sizes B, D, E, F and G**: (K 2, P 2) to 2 sts before marker, sl 1, K 1, psso, SM, K 2, K 2 tog, P 2, (K 2, P 2) to end.

5th round: **Sizes A and C**: (P 2, K 2) to 3 sts before marker, P 1, P 2 tog, SM, K 2, P 2 tog, P 1, K 2, (P 2, K 2) to end. **Sizes B, D, E, F and G**: (K 2, P 2) to 5 sts before marker, K 2, P 1, P 2 tog, SM, K 2, P 2 tog, P 1, (K 2, P 2) to end.*

Rep from * to * once. Cast off loosely in rib.

Making up

Darn in loose ends. Press if desired.

Saddle-shoulder Sweater

First make a tension sample (see page 10) and take measurements (see page 11).

Next choose stitch patterns for the body and for the shoulder saddle and sleeve. The pattern for the saddle and sleeve should be wide enough to cover most of the width of the saddle. If you wish to use an allover pattern for the body, choose one which can be repeated in a round. This should be a fairly simple pattern over no more than about ten stitches. If you choose a lace pattern you can work out the number of sts on the basis of your stocking-stitch tension sample. If you decide to use a cable pattern it will be necessary to work a sample in your chosen stitch (see the Design Instructions for the Saddle-shoulder Cardigan on page 52).

The next step is to convert the following measurements into a number of sts, calculated from your tension sample: chest (this number of sts must be a multiple of the number of sts in your body pattern); upper arm; wrist; shoulders.

The calculation of the back neck sts is a little more complex. The object is to ensure that the V-neck shaping ends at the underarm, therefore the first step is to determine the number of rows which will be worked from the first neck shaping to the underarm. For this you will need to plan the sleeve shaping, and before the sleeve shaping is planned it will be necessary to determine the number of sts to be cast on at the underarm.

To calculate the underarm casting on, subtract twice the number of shoulder sts from the number of chest sts and divide the result by 4.

The sleeve cap can now be divided into four separate components: the sleeve top (which will be the shoulder saddle), five rows with increases every row, a number of rows with increases every alternate row, and the underarm cast ons.

First determine the number of rows in the alternate-row increases in the sleeve cap shaping. From the total number of sts in the upper arm measurement subtract the number of sts in the sleeve top (one-third of the upper-arm sts minus 10), the underarm cast-ons, and 10 (the number of sts added in the every-row increases). The reason for subtracting 10 from the sleeve-top sts and adding 10 sts in every-row increases is to give the sleeve top a more smoothly rounded shape. This will give the number of sts to be added in the alternate row increases, and as there are 2 sts added every second row, it will also give the number of rows in the alternate-row increases.

To obtain the total number of rows in the sleeve cap shapings, add 5 to the number of rows in the alternate-row increases.

The neck increases begin on the second row of the sleeve cap shapings (the first sleeve cap shaping row is on the wrong side of the work) and are done every fourth row. If you divide the number of rows in the sleeve cap shaping by 4, it will give you the number of sts which will be added on each side of the neck shaping. Multiply this figure by 2 and you will have the back neck sts. (Or, more simply, divide the number of rows in the sleeve cap shaping by 2.)

Shoulder saddles

The number of sts in the shoulder saddles is the number of sleeve top sts previously calculated minus 12 (the number of every-row increases plus two extra sts which will be picked up at a later stage).

Choose a lace pattern which consists of one or two less than this number of sts. This pattern will continue down the sleeve to the wrist.

Next calculate the number of rows in the saddle. From the number of sts for the shoulder measurement subtract the back neck sts and divide the result by 2. To convert this number of sts into rows, divide it by 2 and multiply the result by 3.

Invisibly cast on the calculated number of saddle sts and work the calculated number of rows. Leave the sts on a stitch-holder and work another saddle to correspond.

Back

Next calculate the number of sts required for the shoulder side (shoulder sts minus back neck sts divided by 2). Using a circular needle, pick up this number evenly along one side of one shoulder saddle, starting at the stitch-holder end. Invisibly cast on the calculated number of back neck sts, then pick up the number of sts for the shoulder side along the side of the other shoulder saddle, starting at the cast-on end. Purl 1 row.

Now shape the shoulders. Work across the right shoulder and back neck sts, then work one-third of the left shoulder sts and turn (see page 11). Purl back across the left shoulder and neck sts, purl one-third of the right shoulder sts and turn. Knit back to left shoulder, knit two-thirds of the sts and turn. Continue in this manner until all the sts have been knitted up. Break off yarn and leave sts on the circular needle.

Front

Join in yarn at stitch-holder end of right shoulder saddle. Using the same circular needle, with right side of work facing, pick up the calculated number of shoulder side sts evenly along side. Using a second ball of yarn, join in yarn at cast-on end of left shoulder saddle and pick up the same number of sts evenly along side.

Purl 1 row on both sides, then shape the shoulders in the same manner as given for the back. Finish with a purl row across both fronts. Break off yarn from right front and slip right-front sts onto the right-hand end of the circular needle.

Sleeve top and neck shaping

Begin your lace pattern in the first row. Draw a diagram of the front of the sweater and work out where the beginning of the pattern should occur in your first row. Make allowances for the extra sts which will be added in the body shaping and the underarm casting on (see below) in order to ensure that the pattern will continue smoothly over the whole of the body after the sleeves have been worked.

First work across left front, *PM, knit up 1 st from side edge, work sts from stitch-holder, knit up 1 st from edge of back, PM*, work across back, rep from * to *, work across right front.

Work 5 rows, increasing on the armhole sides of the markers in every row, and on neck edge in next and every 4th row. Continue increasing at the neck edges until you have added half the number of back neck sts on each side of the front, then work 3 more rows without shaping at neck edge, then join the work together and work from here on in rounds.

After working the 5 rows with the increases in every row, continue increasing at armhole markers every alternate round.

At this point make another calculation. The previously calculated number of sts will have to be added at the underarm, and the body will have to be shaped at the bottom of the armhole. The number of sts to be added in the body shaping on each side of each armhole will be half the number of underarm cast-ons.

Continue the alternate row increases on the armhole until the number of sleeve sts equals the number of sts calculated for the upper arm minus the calculated number of underarm cast-ons and twice the calculated number of body increases. Continue the sleeve cap increases as before, at the same time increasing also on the body sides of the markers for the number of times you have calculated for the body increases, the last body increase coinciding with the last armhole increase.

Sleeves

Work 1 more round, then break off yarn and slip left-front sts (to marker) onto right-hand needle point. Using a set of double-pointed needles, work across sleeve sts then invisibly cast on the number of sts which you have calculated for the underarm cast ons. Place half the cast-on sts on the first double-pointed needle and half on the third. Work in rounds for 5 cm, then decrease at each end of every 4th or 6th round until the sleeve is the required length minus 5 cm.

In order to work out the decreasing intervals so that the sleeve will be the correct length, first calculate the number of rows in the shaped part of the sleeve (sleeve length minus 10 cm). Subtract the wrist sts from the upper arm sts and divide the result by 2. This will give you the number of decreasing rows. Divide the calculated number of rows in the shaped part of the sleeve first by 4 and then by 6. Choose whichever result is closest to the number of wrist sts but not less than that number. On the last round, decrease any excess sts evenly over the round so that the final number is equal to the number of sts required for the wrist.

Change to smaller sized double-pointed needles and work 5 cm in rib.

Join in yarn at left-front end of underarm casting on, work across cast-on sts then work across back to next marker. Work another sleeve to correspond.

Body

Join in yarn at right-back end of underarm casting on. Work across the cast-on sts then work the front sts. Continue working in rounds until the body is the desired length minus 8 cm.

Change to smaller sized circular needle and work in rib for 8 cm. If you wish to work the band in K 2, P 2 rib, make sure that the number of sts is divisible by 4. If it is not, decrease the appropriate number of sts evenly over the last round before the ribbing.

Neckband

With smaller sized double-pointed needles, knit up neck sts from invisible casting on on neck and left shoulder saddle. Pick up 3 sts for every 4 rows down left side. If you are going to work the band in K 1, P 1 rib, place a marker at this point then pick up 1 st from the centre of the V. If you are going to work the band in K 2, P 2 rib, first make sure that the number of sts is divisible by 4, then place a marker before the last 2 sts picked up on the side (centre of V). To ensure that these 2 centre sts are knit sts it may be necessary to begin the rounds with P 2 instead of K 2. Pick up the same number of sts on the right side and divide the sts onto 3 needles. Work in rib until the band is desired width, decreasing before and after the marker in every round if working in K 1, P 1 rib. If working in K 2, P 2 rib, work the decreases before the marker, then K 2 and decrease again. Cast off loosely in rib.

Making up

Darn in loose ends. Press if desired.

Dolman sweater with squared pattern (page 30)

Vertical striped cotton jacket (page 62); detail above

Raglan school sweaters, knitted in 8-ply on the left (page 67) and in 5-ply on the right (page 69)

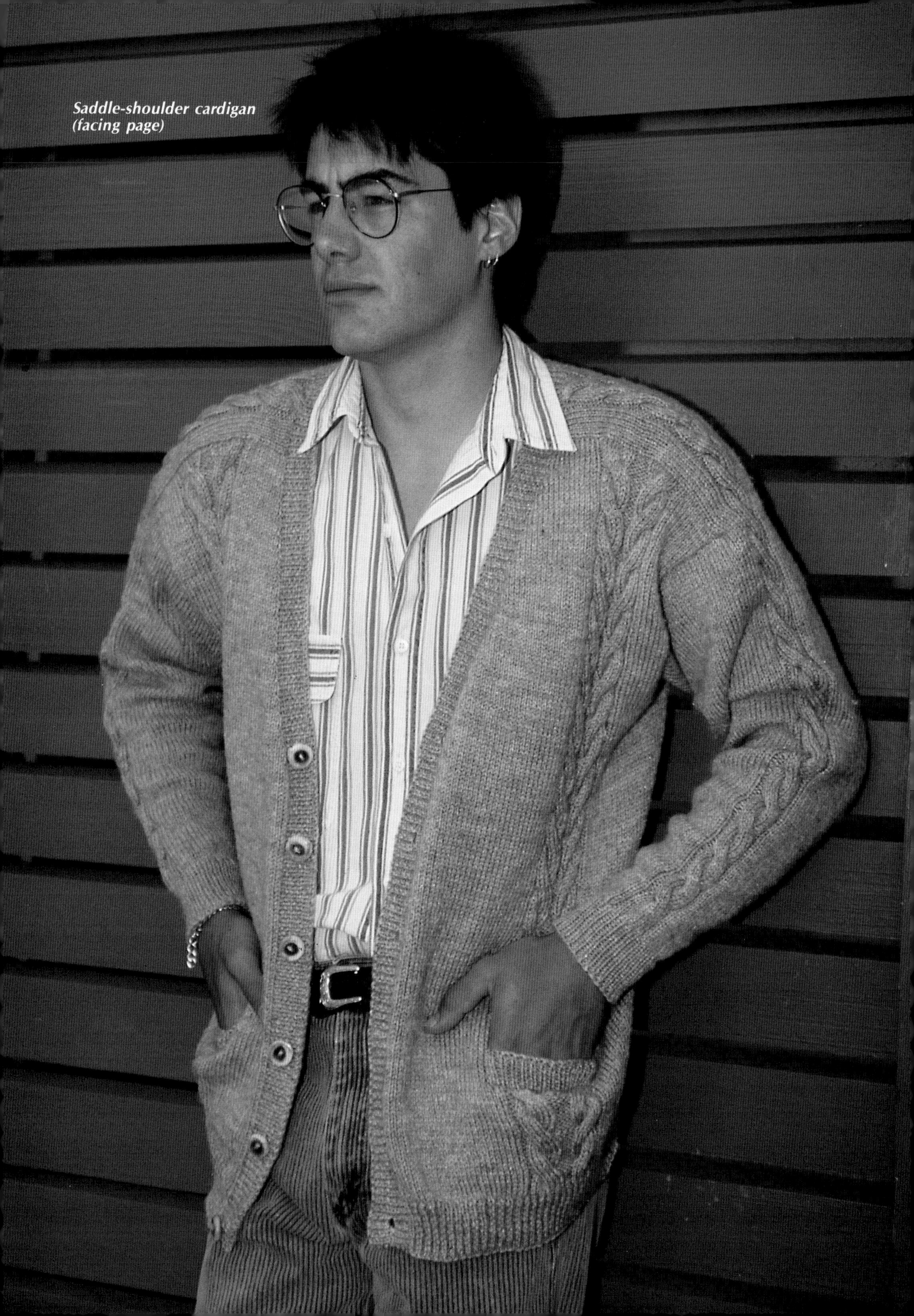

Saddle-shoulder cardigan (facing page)

Saddle-shoulder Cardigan

Illustrated on facing page

This cardigan features a square-set sleeve and a saddle shoulder with a simple eight-stitch cable continuing down the sleeve. The front and back feature a double cable design. The seamless pockets are not stitched down to the front.

Fits chest size (cm)

A	B	C	D	E	F	G
90	95	**100**	105	**110**	115	**120**

Measures (cm)

100	105	**110**	115	**120**	125	**130**

Sleeve length, underarm to wrist (cm)

45	47	**48**	49	**50**	51	**52**

Materials

50 gm balls of 8-ply yarn
14: 15: **16**: 17: **18**: 19: **19** balls
80 cm circular needles and sets of four double-pointed needles in sizes 4 mm and 3.25 mm
Cable needle
2 stitch-holders
6 buttons
Small quantity of left-over yarn

Tension

22 sts and 30 rows to 10 cm, measured over stocking stitch, using 4 mm needles.

Special abbreviations

C8F: Slip next 4 sts onto cable needle and hold in front of work. Knit next 4 sts then knit sts from cable needle.
C8B: Slip next 4 sts onto cable needle and hold at back of work. Knit next 4 sts then knit sts from cable needle.

INSTRUCTIONS

The first step is to work the two shoulder saddles. Using 4 mm needles (or circular needle), invisibly cast on **24**: 24: **24**: 26: **26**: 28: **28** sts.
1st row: K **6**: 6: **6**: 7: **7**: 8: **8**, P 2, K 8, P 2, K **6**: 6: **6**: 7: **7**: 8: **8**.
2nd row: P **6**: 6: **6**: 7: **7**: 8: **8**, K 2, P 8, K 2, P **6**: 6: **6**: 7: **7**: 8: **8**.
*3rd row: K **6**: 6: **6**: 7: **7**: 8: **8**, P 2, C8F, P 2, K **6**: 6: **6**: 7: **7**: 8: **8**.
4th row: As 2nd row.
Rep 1st and 2nd rows 4 times.*
Rep from * to * until **58**: 58: **58**: 71: **71**: 71: **71** rows have been completed from the beginning of the work.
Break off yarn and leave sts on a stitch-holder. Work another saddle to correspond, working cables as C8B.
Now begin the back. Using 4 mm circular needle, with right side of work facing, pick up **42**: 44: **46**: 47: **50**: 52: **55** sts evenly along long side of one shoulder saddle, starting at stitch-holder end.
Invisibly cast on **32**: 34: **36**: 38: **38**: 40: **40** sts, then pick up **42**: 44: **46**: 47: **50**: 52: **55** sts evenly along long side of second shoulder saddle, starting at cast-on end (**116**: 122: **128**: 132: **138**: 144: **150** sts).
1st row: P **9**: 10: **11**: 12: **13**: 14: **16**, **K 2, P 8, K 4, P 8, K 2**, P **50**: 54: **58**: 60: **64**: 68: **70**, rep from * to *,P **9**: 10: **11**: 12: **13**: 14: **16**.

2nd row: K **9**: 10: **11**: 12: **13**: 14: **16**, P 2, K 8, P 4, K 8, P 2, K **50**: 54: **58**: 60: **64**: 68: **70**, P 2, K **3**: 2: **3**: 2: **1**: 2: **2**, turn (see page 00).

3rd row: P **3**: 2: **3**: 2: **1**: 2: **2**, K 2, P **50**: 54: **58**: 60: **64**: 68: **70**, K 2, P **3**: 2: **3**: 2: **1**: 2: **2**, turn.

4th row: K **3**: 2: **3**: 2: **1**: 2: **2**, P 2, K **50**: 54: **58**: 60: **64**: 68: **70**, P 2, K 8, P 4, K **5**: 5: **6**: 6: **6**: 7: **8**, turn.

5th row: P **5**: 5: **6**: 6: **6**: 7: **8**, K 4, P 8, K 2, P **50**: 54: **58**: 60: **64**: 68: **70**, K 2, P 8, K 4, P **5**: 5: **6**: 6: **6**: 7: **8**, turn.

6th row: K **5**: 5: **6**: 6: **6**: 7: **8**, P 4, K 8, P 2, K **50**: 54: **58**: 60: **64**: 68: **70**, P 2, K 8, P 4, K 8, P 2, K **9**: 10: **11**: 12: **13**: 14: **16**.

***7th row:* As 1st row.

8th row: K **9**: 10: **11**: 12: **13**: 14: **16**, *P 2, C8F, P 4, C8B, P 2*, K **50**: 54: **58**: 60: **64**: 68: **70**, rep from * to *, K **9**: 10: **11**: 12: **13**: 14: **16**.

9th row: As 1st row.

10th row: K **9**: 10: **11**: 12: **13**: 14: **16**, *P 2, K 8, P 4, K 8, P 2*, K **50**: 54: **58**: 60: **64**: 68: **70**, rep from * to *, K **9**: 10: **11**: 12: **13**: 14: **16**.

Rep 9th and 10th rows 3 times.**

Rep from ** to ** until **67**: 69: **69**: 71: **71**: 73: **73** rows have been completed from the beginning.

Break off yarn, thread sts onto a length of left-over yarn.

Front shoulders

Join in yarn at stitch-holder end of right shoulder saddle. Using the same circular needle, with right side of work facing, pick up **42**: 44: **46**: 47: **50**: 52: **55** sts evenly along side. Using a second ball of yarn, join in yarn to cast-on end of left shoulder saddle and pick up **42**: 44: **46**: 47: **50**: 52: **55** sts evenly along side.

1st row: Left front: P **9**: 10: **11**: 12: **13**: 14: **16**, K 2, P 8, K 4, P 8, K 2, P **9**: 10: **11**: 11: **13**: 14: **15**. Right front: P **9**: 10: **11**: 11: **13**: 14: **15**, K 2, P 8, K 4, P 8, K 2, P **9**: 10: **11**: 12: **13**: 14: **16**.

2nd row: Right front: K **9**: 10: **11**: 12: **13**: 14: **16**, P 2, K 8, P 4, K 8, P 2, K **9**: 10: **11**: 11: **13**: 14: **15**. Left front: K **9**: 10: **11**: 11: **13**: 14: **15**, P 2, K **3**: 2: **3**: 2: **1**: 2: **2**, turn.

3rd row: Left front: P **3**: 2: **3**: 2: **1**: 2: **2**, K 2, P **9**: 10: **11**: 11: **13**: 14: **15**. Right front: P **9**: 10: **11**: 11: **13**: 14: **15**, K 2, P **3**: 2: **3**: 2: **1**: 2: **2**, turn.

4th row: Right front: K **3**: 2: **3**: 2: **1**: 2: **2**, P 2, K **9**: 10: **11**: 11: **13**: 14: **15**. Left front: K **9**: 10: **11**: 11: **13**: 14: **15**, P 2, K 8, P 4, K **5**: 5: **6**: 6: **6**: 7: **8**, turn.

5th row: Left front: P **5**: 5: **6**: 6: **6**: 7: **8**, K 4, P 8, K 2, P **9**: 10: 11: 11: **13**: 14: **15**. Right front: P **9**: 10: **11**: 11: **13**: 14: **15**, K 2, P 8, K 4, P **5**: 5: **6**: 6: **6**: 7: **8**, turn.

6th row: Right front: K **5**: 5: **6**: 6: **6**: 7: **8**, P 4, K 8, P 2, K **9**: 10: **11**: 11: **13**: 14: **15**. Left front: K **9**: 10: **11**: 11: **13**: 14: **15**, P 2, K 8, P 4, K 8, P 2, K **9**: 10: **11**: 12: **13**: 14: **16**.

7th row: Left front: P **9**: 10: **11**: 12: **13**: 14: **16**, K 2, P 8, K 4, P 8, K 2, P **9**: 10: **11**: 11: **13**: 14: **15**. Right front: P **9**: 10: **11**: 11: **13**: 14: **15**, K 2, P 8, K 4, P 8, K 2, P **9**: 10: **11**: 12: **13**: 14: **16**.

8th row: Right front: K **9**: 10: **11**: 12: **13**: 14: **16**, P 2, C8F, P 4, C8B, P 2, K **8**: 9: **10**: 11: **12**: 13; **15**, inc 1, K 1. Left front: K 1, inc 1, K **8**: 9: **10**: 11: **12**: 13; **15**, P 2, C8F, P 4, C8B, K **9**: 10: **11**: 12: **13**: 14: **16**.

Keeping cable pattern correct and increasing 1 st at neck edge every 4th row, continue until **67**: 69: **69**: 71: **71**: 73: **73** rows have been worked from beginning (**57**: 60: **62**: 63: **66**: 69: **72** sts each side).

Break off yarn and thread sts onto a length of left-over yarn.

Left sleeve

Using 4 mm circular needle, with right side of work facing, beginning at lower edge of left front, pick up **44**: 45: **45**: 46: **46**: 48: **48** sts evenly along back armhole edge. (Pick up 2 sts for every 3 rows.) Keeping cable pattern correct, work sts from left shoulder saddle, then pick up **44**: 45: **45**: 46: **46**: 48: **48** sts evenly along front armhole edge (**112**: 114: **114**: 118: **118**: 124: **124** sts). Divide sts onto three 4 mm double-pointed needles.

Work 12 rows without shaping, then join work together and knit in rounds.

Work without shaping until sleeve measures 5 cm from the point where it was joined into a round.
Next round: K 1, K 2 tog, work to last 3 sts, sl 1, K 1, psso, K 1.

Decrease in this manner every 4th round until **58**: 58: **56**: 58: **58**: 60: **60** sts remain.

Work 3 rounds without shaping.
Next round: Decrease **10**: 8: **2**: 2: **0**: 2: **0** sts evenly over round (**48**: 50: **54**: 56: **58**: 60: **60** sts).

Change to 3.25 mm double-pointed needles and work in K 1, P 1 rib for 5 cm. Cast off loosely in rib.

Right sleeve

Work as for left sleeve.

Body

Replace front and back sts on the 4 mm circular needle. Rejoin yarn at left centre front and knit across left front, keeping cable pattern correct. Knit up **16**: 16: **15**: 17: **16**: 16: **15** sts along unjoined edges of left sleeve, work across back, knit up **16**: 16: **15**: 17: **16**: 16: **15** sts along unjoined edges of right sleeve, then work across right front (**262**: 274: **282**: 292: **302**: 314: **324** sts).

Keeping cable pattern correct, continue working in rows and increasing at neck edge **1**: 1: **2**: 3: **3**: 3: **3** more times, until body is desired length minus

15 cm, ending with a wrong-side row halfway between cables.

Next row: K **23**: 25: **27**: 29: **30**: 32: **34**. *Using a piece of contrasting yarn, K 28, then slip these sts back onto the left-hand needle point. Work across these contrasting st in cable pattern.* K **162**: 170: **176**: 184: **192**: 200: **206**, rep from * to *, K **23**: 25: **27**: 29: **30**: 32: **34**.

Work 10 cm more, ending with a wrong-side row.

Change to 3.25 mm circular needle and work in K 1, P 1 rib for 5 cm. Cast off loosely in rib.

Pockets

Carefully pull out contrasting yarn. Using 4 mm double-pointed needles, with right sides facing, pick up 28 sts from bottom of slit, 1 st at side, 28 sts at top of slit, and 1 st at side. (*Note:* This procedure is safer and easier if a smaller sized needle is threaded through the sts to be picked up before the contrasting yarn is pulled out.) Divide the sts onto 3 needles and work 10 cm in st-st. Divide again onto 2 needles (top sts on one needle, bottom sts on the other) and carefully turn pockets inside out. With needles side by side, right sides of work together, using a third needle, knit the first sts on the back and front needles together, then knit the second sts and cast off the first. Continue in this manner until all the sts are cast off. Fold pocket down.

Using 3.25 mm needles, pick up 28 sts along top of fold, taking care to keep an even line. Work 8 rows in K 1, P 1 rib. At the end of each row pick up 1 st from the body close to the pocket top and knit it together with the last st. Cast off loosely in rib.

Band

Using 3.25 mm circular needle, with right side of work facing and starting at lower edge of right front, pick up 1 st for each row up right side to last neck increase, then 3 sts for every 4 rows along shaped edge. Knit up **24**: 24: **24**: 26: **26**: 28: **28** sts from right saddle invisible casting on, then **32**: 34: **36**: 38: **38**: 40: **40** sts from back neck invisible casting on and **24**: 24: **24**: 26: **26**: 28: **28** sts from left saddle casting on. Pick up 3 sts for every 4 rows along shaped edge of left front, then 1 st for each row to bottom edge.

Work 4 rows in K 1, P 1 rib.

Next row: Rib 4, cast off 3 sts for buttonhole. Work 5 more buttonholes evenly spaced between bottom edge and beginning of neck shaping (see Placing Buttonholes, page 14).

Next row: Rib to 1st buttonhole. Cast on 3 sts over each buttonhole.

Work 4 more rows in rib. Cast off loosely in rib.

Making up

Darn in loose ends. Sew on buttons. Press if desired.

Saddle-shoulder Cardigan

First make a tension sample in st-st (see page 10) and take measurements (see page 11).

If you intend to use a cable pattern for this design, you will need to make a second sample. The reason for this is that cables need a few more sts for a given measurement than plain st-st.

Choose a pattern for your sleeve cable. Cast on the required number of sts, allowing 2 purl sts on either side of the cable, plus about 20 sts on each side of the pattern. For example: If your cable takes 8 sts, you will need 12 sts for the cable pattern, plus 20 each side, making a total of 52 sts. Work three or four pattern repeats (at least 5 cm in length).

Choose a pattern for the front and back (or the front only if you would like the back to be plain). This pattern should be no more than 10 cm in width. Work another sample in the same manner.

From these samples, calculate how many more sts will be needed for 10 cm than for ordinary st-st.

Shoulder saddles

Decide how wide you would like the shoulder saddles to be (usually a little less than one-third of the upper arm measurement). Invisibly cast on the appropriate number of sts calculated from the st-st tension sample, plus the number of extra sts which you will need for the cable pattern. Work in your chosen pattern until the saddle is the length of your shoulder measurement, from the side of the neck to the top of the sleeve. Break off yarn and place the sts on a stitch-holder.

Work another saddle to correspond.

Back shoulders

From your shoulder measurement subtract the length of the two shoulder saddles. This will give you the back neck measurement. Using your stitch tension, convert this measurement into a number of sts.

Take one shoulder saddle and, starting at the stitch-holder end, pick up along the side 2 sts to every 3 rows. Using the same yarn, invisibly cast on the number of sts calculated for the back neck. Take the other shoulder saddle and, starting at the cast-on end, pick up the same number of sts along the side as for the first shoulder saddle. Count the sts. Before going any further, calculate the number of sts required for your shoulder measurement, plus any extra sts needed for your cable pattern. If you do not have this number of sts on your needle, you may need to make an adjustment at this stage. Work 1 row.

The next step is to shape the shoulders. (This step may be omitted if a straight shoulder is desired.) Work across the left shoulder and neck, then work one-third of the right shoulder sts and turn (see page 11). Work back across these sts and the neck sts, then work one-third of the left shoulder sts and turn. Work back to right shoulder and work two-thirds of the sts and turn. Continue in this manner until all the sts have been knitted up.

Work until the back and half the shoulder saddle measure half your upper arm measurement.

Break off yarn, thread sts onto a length of left-over yarn.

Front shoulders

Join in yarn at stitch-holder end of right shoulder saddle. Using the same circular needle, with right side of work facing, pick up evenly along the side the same number of sts as for the back. Using a second ball of yarn, join in yarn to cast-on end of left shoulder saddle and pick up the same number of sts evenly along the side.

Work shoulder shapings to correspond with the back.

Work a few rows without shaping, then commence the neck shaping. Increase 1 st at neck edge in every 4th row until the number of sts on each front equals half the number of back sts (in other words, the number of sts added to each front equals half the back neck sts).

When the fronts are the same length as the back, break off yarn and thread sts onto a length of leftover yarn.

Sleeves

First calculate from your stitch tension the number of sts required for the upper arm measurement, adding in any extra sts needed for the cable pattern. Subtract the number of sts in the saddle from this number, then divide the result by 2. This gives the number of sts to be picked up along the side of the fronts and back.

Using double-pointed needles, with right side of work facing and starting at bottom edge of left front, pick up the previously calculated number of sts along the side of the front. If the measurements and calculations are correct, this should come to approximately 2 sts for every 3 rows. Work across the saddle sts then pick up the same number of sts along the side of the back.

Before going any further, calculate the number of sts required for the chest measurement, adding in any extra needed for the cable pattern. Subtract the total number of sts now on the back and the fronts and divide the result by 2. This will give the number of sts to be added to complete the body.

Convert this figure from sts into rows by dividing it by 2 and multiplying the result by 3, then divide this again by 2. For example: Sts required to complete the body = 20; divide by 2 = 10; multiply by 3 = 30; divide by 2 = 15.

Work this calculated number of rows without shaping, then join the sleeve st together and work in rounds.

Work about 5 cm without shaping, then decrease at each end of every 4th or 6th round until the sleeve is 5 cm less than the desired length.

To work out the correct decreasing intervals so that the sleeve will be the correct length, first calculate the number of rows in the shaped part of the sleeve (sleeve length minus 10 cm). Subtract the wrist sts from the upper arm sts and divide the result by 2. This will give you the number of decreasing rows. Divide the calculated number of rows in the shaped part of the sleeve first by 4 and then by 6. Choose whichever result is closest to the number of wrist sts but not less than that number.

The calculated number of sts required for the wrist should not include any extra sts for the cable pattern. Subtract that number from the number of sts still on the needles. On the last round before working the cuff, decrease the excess number evenly over the round.

Change to smaller sized needles and work 5 cm in rib. Cast off loosely in rib.

Body

Replace front and back sts on the circular needle. Rejoin yarn at left centre front and work across left front. Pick up along unjoined edges of left sleeve half the calculated number of sts required to complete the body. This should work out at 2 sts for every 3 rows. Work across back then pick up the same number of sts along unjoined edge of right sleeve and work across right front.

Continue working in rows until the body is the desired length minus 15 cm, ending with a wrong-side row.

The next step is to knit in a piece of contrasting yarn for later placing of the pockets. The pocket should be approximately 10 cm in width and should correspond with the cable pattern on the fronts. Decide on the position of the pocket, then work up to that point. Using a piece of contrasting yarn, knit across the pocket sts then slip these sts back onto the left-hand needle. Work across these sts in pattern. Work right front to correspond.

Work another 10 cm, ending with a wrong-side row.

Change to smaller sized circular needle and work in rib for 5 cm. Cast off loosely in rib.

Pockets

Carefully pull out contrasting yarn. Using double-pointed needles, with right sides facing, pick up the same number of sts as worked on the contrasting yarn from bottom of slit, 1 st at side, the same number of sts at top of slit, and 1 st at side. (Note: This procedure is safer and easier if a smaller sized needle is threaded through the sts to be picked up before the contrasting yarn is pulled out.) Divide the sts on to 3 needles and work 10 cm in st-st. Divide again onto 2 needles (top sts on one needle, bottom sts on the other) and carefully turn pockets inside out. With needles side by side, right sides of work together, using a third needle, knit the first sts on the back and front needles together, then knit the second sts and cast off the first. Continue in this manner until all the sts are cast off. Fold pocket down.

Using smaller sized needles, pick up the number of pocket sts along top of fold, taking care to keep an even line. Work 8 rows in rib. At the end of each row, pick up 1 st from the body close to the pocket top and knit it together with the last st. Cast off loosely in rib.

Band

Using smaller sized circular needle, with right side of work facing and starting at lower edge of right front, pick up 1 st for each row up right side to last neck increase, then 3 sts for every 4 rows along shaped edge. Knit up sts from invisible casting on on right saddle, back neck and left saddle. Pick up 3 sts for every 4 rows along shaped edge of left front, then 1 st for each row to bottom edge.

Work 10 rows in rib, working buttonholes at regular intervals between bottom edge and beginning of neck shaping in 5th and 6th rows. Cast off loosely in rib.

Making up

Darn in loose ends. Sew on buttons. Press if desired.

PATTERN

Traditional Aran Sweater

Illustrated on page 57

Traditional Aran designs are attractive and simpler to knit than they appear. This sweater features a wide, complex cable design in the centre of the body with a 'cupped cable' panel on either side, flanked by a simple four-stitch cable. The saddle-shoulder sleeves feature a five-fold Aran braid design. The rest of the sweater is worked in double moss stitch. It is worked from the bottom to the shoulders; the shoulder saddles are then worked and the sleeves knitted from the top down.

Fits chest size (cm)

A	B	C	D	E	F	G
90	95	**100**	105	**110**	115	**120**

Measures (cm)

100	105	**110**	115	**120**	125	**130**

Sleeve length, underarm to wrist (cm)

45	47	**48**	49	**50**	51	**52**

Materials

50 gm balls of 8-ply yarn
22: 24: **55**: 26: **27**: 29: **30** balls
80 cm circular needles and sets of four double-pointed needles in sizes 4 mm and 3.25 mm
Cable needle
2 stitch-holders
Small quantity of left-over yarn

Tension

22 sts and 30 rows to 10 cm, measured over stocking stitch, using 4 mm needles.

Special abbreviations

C4F: Slip next 2 sts onto cable needle and hold in front of work. Knit next 2 sts then knit sts from cable needle.
C4B: Slip next 2 sts onto cable needle and hold at back of work. Knit next 2 sts then knit sts from cable needle.
T5L: Slip next 2 sts onto cable needle and hold at front of work, K 2, P 1, K 2 from cable needle.
T3B: Slip next st onto cable needle and hold at back of work, K 2, P st from cable needle.
T3F: Slip next 2 sts onto cable needle and hold at front of work, P 1, then K 2 from cable needle.
Cr5F: Slip next 3 sts onto cable needle and hold at front of work, K 2, slip P st back onto left-hand needle and P it, K 2 from cable needle.
Cr5B: Slip next 3 sts onto cable needle and hold at back of work, K 2, slip P st back onto left-hand needle and P it, K 2 from cable needle.

Centre panel multi-cable stitch pattern

This panel consists of 49 sts and 28 rows.
1st row: (P 2, K 4) 4 times, P 1, (K 4, P 2) 4 times.
2nd and alternate (even-numbered) rows: K the K sts and P the P sts as they present.
3rd row: *P 2, C4F, P 2, K 4*, rep from * to *, P 1, *K 4, P 2, C4B, P 2*, rep from * to *.
5th row: As 1st row.
7th row: P 2, C4F, P 2, K 4, P 2, C4F, P 2, slip next 5 sts onto cable needle and hold at front of work, K 4, then slip the P st back onto left-hand needle and P it, K 4 from cable needle, P 2, C4B, P 2, K 4, P 2, C4B, P 2.
9th row: P 2, K 4, P 2, *inc 1 p, (K 4, P 2) twice, K 4, inc 1 P*, P 1, rep from * to *, P 2, K 4, P 2.
11th row: P 2, C4F, P 3, inc 1 p, K 4, P 2 tog, C4F, P 2 tog, K 4, inc 1 P, P 3, inc 1 P, K 4, P 2 tog, C4B, P 2 tog, K 4, inc 1 P, P 3, C4B, P 2.

13th row: P 2, K 4, P 4, *inc 1 P, K 3, sl 1, K 1, psso, K 4, K 2 tog, K 3, inc 1 P*, P 5, rep from * to *, P 4, K 4, P 2.
15th row: P 2, C4F, P 5, inc 1 P, K 4, C4F, K 4, inc 1 P, P 7, inc 1 P, K 4, C4B, K 4, inc 1 P, P 5, C4B, P 2.
17th row: P 2, K 4, P 6, slip next 8 sts onto cable needle and hold at back of work, K 4, slip last 4 sts from cable needle back onto left-hand needle and K them, K 4 from cable needle, P 9, slip next 8 sts onto cable needle and hold at front of work, K 4, slip last 4 sts from cable needle back onto left-hand needle and K them, K 4 from cable needle, P 6, K 4, P 2.
19th row: P 2, C4F, P 4, P 2 tog, K 4, C4F, K 4, P 2 tog, P 5, P 2 tog, K 4, C4B, K 4, p 2 tog, P 4, C4B, P 2.
21st row: P 2, K 4, P 3, *P 2 tog, (K 4, inc 1 P) twice, K 4, P 2 tog, P 3*, rep from * to *, K 4, P 2.
23rd row: P 2, C4F, P 2, P 2 tog, K 4, inc 1 P, P 1, C4F, P 1, inc 1 P, K 4, P 2 tog, P 1, P 2 tog, K 4, inc 1 P, P 1, C4B, P 1, inc 1 P, K 4, P 2 tog, P 2, C4B, P 2.
25th row: P 2, K 4, P 1, P 2 tog, *(K 4, P 2) twice, K 4*, P 3 tog, rep from * to *, P 2 tog, P 1, K 4, P 2.
27th row: As 7th row.

Chevron and cable pattern for side panels

This pattern consists of 23 sts and 12 rows.

Left side panel
1st row: P 2, K 4, P 7, T5L, P 5.
2nd and alternate (even-numbered) rows: K the K sts and P the P sts as they present.
3rd row: P 2, C4F, P 6, T3B, K 1, T3F, P 4.
5th row: P 2, K 4, P 5, T3B, K 1, P 1, K 1, T3F, P 3.
7th row: P 2, C4F, P 4, T3B, (K 1, P 1) twice, K 1, T3F, P 2.
9th row: P 2, K 4, P 3, T3B, (K 1, P 1) 3 times, K 1, T3F, P 1.
11th row: P 2, C4F, P 2, T3B, (K 1, P 1) 4 times, K 1, T3F.

Right side panel
1st row: P 5, T5L, P 7, K 4, P 2.
2nd and alternate (even-numbered) rows: K the K sts and P the P sts as they present.
3rd row: P 4, T3B, K 1, T3F, P 6, C4B, P 2.
5th row: P 3, T3B, K 1, P 1, K 1, T3F, P 5, K 4, P 2.
7th row: P 2, T3B, (K 1, P 1) twice, K 1, T3F, P 4, C4B, P 2.
9th row: P 1, T3B, (K 1, P 1) 3 times, K 1, T3F, P 3, K 4, P 2.
11th row: T3B, (K 1, P 1) 4 times, K 1, T3F, P 2, C4B, P 2.

Braid pattern for saddle and sleeve

This pattern consists of 26 sts and 8 rows.
1st and alternate (odd-numbered) rows: (wrong side): (K 1, P 1) twice, K 2, (P 2, K 1) 4 times, P 2, K 2, (P 1, K 1) twice.
2nd row: P 1, K 3, P 2, (K 2, P 1) 4 times, K 2, P 2, K 3, P 1.
4th row: P 1, K 3, P 2, K 2, (P 1, Cr5F) twice, P 2, K 3, P 1.
6th row: As 2nd row.
8th row: P 1, K 3, P 2, (Cr5B, P 1) twice, K 2, P 2, K 3, P 1.

Double moss stitch

1st row: (K 1, P 1) to end of panel.
2nd row: K the K sts and P the P sts as they present.
3rd row: P the K sts and K the P sts as they present.
4th row: As 2nd row.

INSTRUCTIONS

Using 3.25 mm circular needle, cast on **220**: 232: **244**: 252: **264**: 276: **284** sts by the thumb method (see page 11). Place a marker at the beginning of the round and at the half-way mark.
Work 8 cm in K 2, P 2 rib.
Next round: *Rib **24**: 29: **30**: 30: **33**: 36: **36**, (rib 2, inc 1) **31**: 29: **31**: 33: **33**: 33: **35** times, rib **24**: 29: **30**: 30: **33**: 36: **36***, rep from * to * (**282**: 290: **306**: 318: **330**: 342: **354** sts).

Change to 4 mm circular needle and begin the Aran pattern.
Next round: *Work **23**: 25: **29**: 32: **35**: 38: **41** sts in double moss, 23 sts in chevron and cable pattern (left side panel), 49 sts in centre panel multi-cable, 23 sts in chevron and cable pattern (right side panel), then **23**: 25: **29**: 32: **35**: 38: **41** sts in double moss*, rep from * to *.

Back

Continue working in pattern until body is desired length to armhole, ending with an even-numbered pattern round.
Next round: Work to half-way marker, turn. Work on these sts until the armhole measures **20**: 20: **20**: 21: **21**: 23: **23** cm. Thread first **44**: 44: **46**: 47: **48**: 49: **50** sts onto a length of left-over yarn, place next **53**: 57: **61**: 65: **69**: 73: **77** sts on a stitch-holder, then thread next **44**: 44: **46**: 47: **48**: 49: **50** sts onto a length of left-over yarn.

*Traditional Aran sweater
(page 55)*

*Detail of multi-cable front
panel (below left) and
braid pattern on sleeve
(below)*

*Raglan dress with geometric
design on body and sleeves
(page 71)*

Front

Work as for back until armhole measures **10**: 10: **10**: 11: **11**: 13: **13** cm, ending with a wrong-side row.
Next row: Work **57**: 59: **61**: 63: **65**: 67: **69**, turn. Work left front on these sts.

Keeping pattern correct, dec 1 st in every alternate row **13**: 14: **15**: 16: **17**: 18: **19** times (**44**: 44: **46**: 47: **48**: 49: **50** sts).

Work without shaping until front measures the same as the back. Thread sts on a length of left-over yarn.

Place centre **27**: 29: **31**: 33: **35**: 37: **39** sts on a stitch-holder and work right side to correspond.

Shoulder saddle

Using two 4 mm double-pointed needles, invisibly cast on 26 sts. Slip front and back left shoulder sts onto 2 double-pointed needles.
1st row: (wrong side): Work in braid pattern for saddle and sleeve, working last st together with first st at neck edge of left front shoulder.
2nd row: Work 2nd row of braid pattern, working last st together with first st at neck edge of back shoulder.

Continue in this manner, working last st of every row together with 1 st from back and front shoulders alternately, until all the shoulder sts are knitted up. Leave sts on needle.

Sleeve

Using 4 mm double-pointed needles and beginning at bottom of left front armhole, pick up **50**: 51: **51**: 54: **54**: 57: **57** sts evenly along side, work across saddle and pick up **50**: 51: **51**: 54: **54**: 57: **57** sts evenly along left back armhole (**126**: 128: **128**: 134: **134**: 140: **140** sts). Divide sts evenly onto 3 needles.

Keeping saddle pattern correct and working the rest of the sleeve sts in double moss stitch and working 2 P sts at beginning and end of saddle pattern, work 5 cm without shaping.
Next round: Decrease 1 st at beginning and end of round.

Continue to decrease in this manner every 4th round until **64**: 62: **60**: 66: **64**: 68: **66** remain.

Work 3 rounds without shaping.
Next round: Decrease **16**: 14: **8**: 10: **8**: 8: **6** sts evenly over round (**48**: 48: **52**: 56: **56**: 60: **60** sts).

Change to 3.25 mm double-pointed needles and work 5 cm in K 2, P 2 rib. Cast off loosely in rib.
Work another saddle and sleeve to correspond.

Neckband

With right side of work facing and using 3.25 mm double-pointed needles, knit up **53**: 57: **61**: 65: **69**: 73: **77** sts from back neck stitch-holder, 26 sts from left shoulder saddle invisible casting on, pick up **14**: 15: **16**: 17: **18**: 21: **22** sts evenly down left side of neck, knit up **27**: 29: **31**: 33: **35**: 37: **39** sts from centre front neck stitch-holder, then pick up **14**: 15: **16**: 17: **18**: 21: **22** sts evenly up right side of neck and 26 sts from right shoulder saddle invisible casting on (**160**: 168: **176**: 184: **192**: 204: **212** sts).

Work 12 rounds in K 2, P 2 rib. Cast off loosely in rib.

Making up

Darn in loose ends. Do not press.

Traditional Aran Sweater

Designing a traditional Aran sweater is an interesting challenge. It takes a little more time and effort but is not difficult.

First make a tension sample in st-st (see page 10) and take measurements (see page 11).

The next step is to choose the stitch patterns. Traditionally Aran sweaters contain two patterns for the body, a wider one for the central panel and a narrower one for the side panels. These may be flanked by narrow cables. The patterns should be separated by two purl sts. A third pattern is used for the sleeve and shoulder saddle. The rest of the garment is made in a background stitch which may be plain st-st or perhaps double moss.

There are a number of good books which give details of Aran stitch patterns, such as *The Harmony Guide to Knitting Stitches*, published by Lyric Books Limited and available in many shops.

First choose the stitches you would like to have for the body and sketch a diagram, including the number of sts in each panel and two purl sts at either side. Add together the total number of sts needed for the front pattern panels. Aran patterns take more sts than st-st for a given measurement, so it will be necessary to work another sample in your chosen sts.

Work out from your st-st tension sample the number of sts for the chest measurement and divide this number by two. Add about 20 more sts and cast on this number of sts for your pattern sample.

Working your pattern panel in the centre of the sample and your background stitch at either side, work a sample which contains two or three repeats of the patterns. It is a good idea to knit up a whole ball of yarn on this sample; this will help in calculating the quantity of yarn you will need to finish the sweater.

Work another sample in the same manner for your saddle and sleeve pattern with approximately 20 sts at either side of the pattern panel and two purl sts between the background and the pattern.

Carefully measure the width of the pattern panels. Pin the sample on to a large cushion or your ironing board to ensure that it is quite flat. Stretch it a little but not too much. It is important that this measurement is accurate. Do the same for the sleeve sample.

Subtract twice the measurement of the body panels from the chest measurement. Using your st-st tension sample, convert the result into stitches. If you are not using st-st for your background stitch, it will be necessary to check the number of sts to 10 cm in that stitch in order to make this calculation.

Divide the calculated number of sts by 4. This is the number of background sts which you will need on each side of your pattern panels for the front and back.

Make a similar calculation for the sleeve panel, using the upper arm measurement to calculate the number of sts at each side of the pattern panel.

Body

The work begins at the bottom of the sweater. Using a smaller sized circular needle, cast on the number of sts to correspond with your chest measurement from the st-st tension sample. Use the thumb method of casting on (see page 11), taking care when you join the sts into a round that there is no twist in the casting on. Place a marker at the beginning of the round and at the half-way mark. Work 8 cm in rib. Note that if you choose to use K 2, P 2 rib you will need to have a number of sts which is divisible by 4.

Now estimate how many extra sts you will need. Add together the number of sts in the pattern panels plus the number of background sts on the two sides of the panel and multiply the result by 2. Subtract the number of sts on the needle from the result. This will give you the number of sts which will have to be added. On the last round of ribbing, increase this number of sts evenly over the whole round.

Change to larger sized circular needle and work in pattern until the sweater is the desired length to the armhole.

Back

Divide the sts in two by working from the first to the second marker and work in rows until the armhole is the desired length minus half the width of the shoulder saddle (measured from the pattern sample).

Estimate the back neck measurement (usually one-third of the shoulder measurement). Measure off this number of sts from the centre of the row. Thread the sts on either side of these sts onto a length of left-over yarn and place the neck sts on a stitch-holder.

Front

Work the front as for the back up to the desired depth of the neck. Subtract half the number of back neck sts from the number of sts on the needle and divide the result by two. Work this number of sts and turn. Working on these sts, decrease at neck edge every alternate row until you have taken off a quarter of the number of back neck sts, then work without shaping until the front is the same length as the back.

Place half the number of back neck sts onto a stitch-holder and complete the right side of the front to correspond.

Shoulder saddle

Invisibly cast on the number of sts for your pattern panel plus 2 (1 purl st at either side).

Slip the front and back left shoulder sts onto 2 double-pointed needles. While working your saddle (beginning at the neck edge), work the last st of every row together with 1 st from the front and back shoulders alternately.

Sleeves

When the saddle is completed, using double-pointed needles and beginning at the bottom edge of the front armhole, pick up half the number of sts calculated for the upper arm minus half the saddle sts, work across the saddle sts and pick up the same number of sts down the back armhole. Divide the sts evenly onto 3 needles.

Work in rounds for 5 cm, then decrease 1 st at each end of every 4th or 6th round until the sleeve is 5 cm less than the desired measurement. Work 3 rounds without shaping.

In order to work out the correct decreasing intervals so that the sleeve will be the correct length, first calculate the number of rows in the shaped part of the sleeve (sleeve length minus 10 cm). Subtract the wrist sts from the upper arm sts and divide the result by 2. This will give you the number of decreasing rows. Divide the calculated number of rows in the shaped part of the sleeve first by 4 and then by 6. Choose whichever result is closest to the number of wrist sts but not less than that number.

Use your st-st tension sample to calculate the number of sts required for the wrist. Subtract this number from the number of sts on the needles. Decrease the resulting number of sts evenly over the next round.

Change to smaller sized double-pointed needles and work 5 cm in rib. Note that if you choose K 2, P 2 rib you will have to ensure that the number of sts is divisible by 4.

Neckband

Using smaller sized double-pointed needles, knit up back neck sts from stitch-holder, saddle sts from invisible casting on, pick up 3 sts for every 4 rows down left neck edge, knit up centre front sts from stitch holder and pick up 3 sts for 4 rows up right neck edge. Check that the number of sts will be even if you are using K 1, P 1 rib or divisible by 4 for K 2, P 2 rib.

Work in rib until band is desired width.

Making up

Darn in loose ends. Do not press.

Vertical-striped Cotton Jacket

Illustrated on page 46

This short-sleeved jacket is knitted sideways, starting at the right sleeve and finishing at the left sleeve. It features multi-coloured and textured stripes and bands worked in moss stitch.

Fits chest size (cm)

A	B	C	D	E
85	90	**95**	100	**105**

Measures (cm)

95	100	**105**	115	**110**

Materials

50 gm balls of 8-ply cotton
First main colour (M1) and second main colour (M2), **3**: 3: **3**: 4: **4** balls each. Small quantities of each of seven other colours (C1 to C7). C3 and C6 should be textured yarns and may be a thicker ply than the main colours. C4 should be a strongly contrasting colour to C3.
80 cm circular needle and a set of four double-pointed needles in size 4 mm
Small quantity of left-over yarn
3 buttons

Tension

22 sts and 36 rows to 10 cm.

INSTRUCTIONS

Begin at the end of the right sleeve. Using M1 and double-pointed needles, cast on **102**: 106: **108**: 108: **112** sts by the thumb method.

1st round: (K 1, P 1) to end.
2nd round: (P 1, K 1) to end.
   Rep these 2 rows 5 times.
   Work striped pattern as follows:
1st round: Using C1, K.
2nd round: Using C1, P.
3rd and 4th rounds: Using M1, K.
5th and 6th rounds: Using C2, K.
7th round: Using M2, K.
8th round: Using C2, K.
9th round: Using M1, K,
   Using M2, K 12 rounds.
22nd round: Using C3 (textured yarn), K.
23rd round: Using C3, P.
24th round: Using C4, K.
25th and 26th rounds: As 22nd and 23rd rounds.
   Using M1, K 7 rounds.
34th round: Using C5, K.
35th round: Using C5, P.
   Using M 1, K 6 rounds.
42nd round: Using M2, K.
43rd round: Using M1, K.
44th and 45th rounds: As 34th and 35th rounds.
   Using M2, K 10 rounds.

Right side of front and back

Transfer sts to circular needle. Still using M2, invisibly cast on **85**: 88: **91**: 93: **94** sts. Knit back across these sts, K the sleeve sts then knit up **85**: 88: **91**: 93: **94** sts from invisible casting on.
1st and 2nd row: Using C6, *(K 1, P 1) 5 times*, K to last 10 sts, rep from * to *.

Continue throughout working first and last 10 sts in each row in moss stitch.
   Using M2, work 5 rows in st-st.
8th and 9th rows: Using C1, K.
   Continue in st-st, working 1 row in M2 and 5 rows in M1.

16th row: Work alternate sts in M1 and C7.
18th and 19th rows: Work M1 sts in C7 and C7 sts in M1.

Work **6**: 8: **8**: 8: **10** more rows in M1.
K 2 rows in C5, then K 1 row in M1.
Work **10**: 10: **14**: 16: **18** rows in M2.
Work 2 rows in C2, K 2 rows in M2, work 2 rows in C2, K 2 rows in M1, work 2 rows in C2, work 4 rows in M1.

Right front shaping

1st row: Using M1, K **123**: 132: **141**: 136: **137**, turn.
2nd row: Using M1, P.
3rd row: Using M1, K **117**: 126: **135**: 131: **132**, turn.
4th row: As 2nd row.
5th row: Using C6, K **111**: 120: **129**: 126: **122**, turn.
6th row: Using C6, K.
7th row: Using M1, K **105**: 114: **123**: 121: **122**, turn.
8th row: Using M1, P.
9th row: Using M2, K **99**: 108: **117**: 116: **117**, turn.
10th row: Using M2, P.
11th row: Using M2, K **93**: 102: **111**: 111: **112**, turn.
12th row: Using M2, P.
13th row: Using M2, K **87**: 96: **105**: 106: **107**, turn.
14th row: **C1**: M2: **M2**: M2: **M2**, **K**: P: **P**: P: **P**.
15th row: Using **C1**: M2: **M2**: M2: **M2**, K **81**: 90: **99**: 101: **102**, turn.
16th row: Using **M2**: C1: **M2**: M2: **M2**, **P**: K: **P**: P: **P**.
17th row: Using **M2**: C1: **M2**: M2: **M2**, K **75**: 84: **93**: 96: **97**, turn.
18th row: Using **C1**: M2: **C1**: M2: **M2**, **K**: P: **K**: P: **P**.
19th row: Using **C1**: M2: **C1**: M2: **M2**, K **69**: 78: **87**: 91: **92**, turn.
20th row: Using **M2**: C1: **M2**: C1: **C1**, **P**: K: **P**: K: **K**.
21st row: Using **M2**: C1: **M2**: C1: **M2**, K **63**: 72: **81**: 86: **87**, turn.
22nd row: Using **M2**: M2: **C1**: M2: **M2**, **P**: P: **K**: P: **P**.
23rd row: Using **0**: M2: **C1**: M2: **M2**, K **0**: 66: **75**: 81: **82**, turn.
24th row: Using **0**: M2: **M2**: C1: **C1**, **0**: P: **P**: K: **K**.
25th row: Using **0**: 0: **M2**: C1: **C1**, K **0**: 0: **69**: 76: **77**, turn.
26th row: Using **0**: 0: **M2**: M2: **M2**, K.
27th row: Using **0**: 0: **0**: M2: **M2**, K **0**: 0: **0**: 71: **72**, turn.
28th row: Using **0**: 0: **0**: M2: **M2**, K.

Centre back

Using M1, work to end of row.
1st row: Using M1, work **136**: 141: **145**: 147: **150**. Thread the rest of the sts on a length of left-over yarn.
2nd row: Using M1, work to end.

Working on these **136**: 141: **145**: 147: **150** sts and keeping continuity of moss stitch border, work stripes as follows:

Using M1, work **0**: 2: **2**: 4: **4** more rows in st-st.
Using C6, K 2 rows.
Using M1, work 2 rows in st-st.
Using M2, work **8**: 8: **10**: 10: **12** rows in st-st.
Using C1, K 2 rows.
Using M2, work 2 rows in st-st.
Using C1, K 2 rows.
Using M2, work 4 rows in st-st.
Using C1, K 2 rows.
Using M2, work 2 rows in st-st.
Using M1, work 4 rows in st-st.
Using C6, K 2 rows.
Using M1, work 2 rows in st-st.
Using C6, K 2 rows.
Using M1, work 2 rows in st-st.
Using C6, K 2 rows.
Using M1, work 2: 4: 4: 6: 6 rows in st-st.

Left front

Using M1, invisibly cast on **136**: 141: **145**: 147: **150** sts.
1st row: Using M2, K **63**: 66: **69**: 71: **72**, turn.
2nd row: Using M2, P.
3rd row: Using C1, K **69**: 72: **75**: 76: **77**, turn.
4th row: Using C1, K.
5th row: Using M2, K **75**: 78: **81**: 81: **82**, turn.
6th row: Using M2, P.
7th row: Using **M1**: M2: **M2**: M2: **M2**, K **81**: 84: **87**: 86: **87**, turn.
8th row: Using **M1**: M2: **M2**: M2: **M2**, P.
9th row: Using **M1**: M1: **M1**: M2: **M2**, K **87**: 90: **93**: 91: **92**, turn.
10th row: Using **M1**: M1: **M1**: M2: **M2**, P.
11th row: Using **C6**: M1: **M1**: M1: **M1**, K **93**: 96: **99**: 96: **97**, turn.
12th row: Using **C6**: M1: **M1**: M1: **M1**, **K**: P: **P**: P: P.
13th row: Using **M2**: C6: **C6**: M1: **M1**, K **99**: 102: **105**: 101: **102**, turn.
14th row: Using **M2**: C6: **C6**: M1: **M1**, **P**: K: **K**: P: **P**.
15th row: Using **M2**: M2: **M2**: C6: **C6**, K **105**: 108: **111**: 106: **107**, turn.
16th row: Using **M2**: M2: **M2**: C6: **C6**, **P**: P: **P**: K: **K**.
17th row: Using **C6**: M2: **M2**: M2: **M2**, K **111**: 114: **117**: 111: **112**, turn.
18th row: Using **C6**: M2: **M2**: M2: **M2**, **K**: P: **P**: P: **P**.
19th row: Using **M1**: C6: **C6**: M2: **M2**, K **117**: 120: **123**: 116: **117**, turn.
20th row: Using **M1**: C6: **C6**: M2: **M2**, **P**: K: **K**: P: **P**.
21st row: Using **M1**: M1: **M1**: C6: **C6**, K **123**: 126: **129**: 121: **122**, turn.
22nd row: Using **M1**: M1: **M1**: C6: **C6**, **P**: P: **P**: K: **K**.
23rd row: Using **0**: M1: **M1**: M1: **M1**, K **0**: 132: **135**: 126: **127**, turn.
24th row: Using **0**: M1: **M1**: M1: **M1**, K.
25th row: Using M1, K **0**: 0: **141**: 131: **132**, turn.
26th row: **Sizes C, D and E**: Using M1, P.

27th row: Using M1, K **0**: 0: **0**: 136: **137**, turn.
28th row: **Sizes D and E:** Using M1, P.

Left side of front and back

1st row: Using M1, work across front and back to end of row.

Work 3 more rows in M1, keeping continuity of moss stitch border.
5th and 6th rows: Using C5, K.
7th row: Using M2, K.
8th row: Using M1, P.

Work 4 rows in M2, 1 row in M1, 1 row in M2 and 1 row in M1, then work **11**: 13: **13**: 15: **15** rows in M2.

Continue stripes as follows:
1st and 2nd rows: Using C3, K.
3rd row: Using C4, K.
4th and 5th rows: Using C3, K.

Work **9**: 11: **11**: 13: **13** rows in M1, then continue as follows:
1st and 2nd rows: Using C1, K.
3rd row: Using M2, K.
4th row: Using M1, P.

Work **6**: 6: **8**: 8: **10** rows in M2, then 1 row in C1.

Left sleeve

Slip **85**: 88: **91**: 93: **94** sts onto a separate needle. Hold this needle alongside the circular needle. Using a third 4 mm needle, P tog the first st on the front and back needle, then P tog the next st. Pass the first st over the second to cast off. Repeat this process until **85**: 88: **91**: 93: **94** sts have been cast off.

Slip sleeve sts onto three double-pointed needles and work in rounds as follows:
1st round: Using C1, P.

Using M2, K 6 rounds.
8th round: Using M1, K.
9th round: Using C1, P.
10th round: Using C1, K.
11th round: Using M2, K.

Using M1, K 10 rounds, then work next stripes as follows:
1st round: Using C6, K.
2nd round: Using C6, P.
3rd round: Using C4, K.
4th round: Using C6, P.
5th round: Using C6, K.

Work 3 rounds in M1 and 10 rounds in M2, then complete striped pattern as follows:
1st round: Using C6, K.
2nd round: Using C6, P.

Work 3 rounds in M2.
6th round: Using M1, K.
7th round: Using M2, K.

Work 3 rounds in M1.
10th round: Using C6, K.
11th round: Using C6, P.

Work 2 rounds in M1.
14th round: Using C6, K.
15th round: Using C6, P.

Work 12 rounds in moss stitch and cast off in moss stitch.

Front band

Using circular needle and M2, knit right front sts from length of yarn, pick up **30**: 32: **33**: 36: **37** sts from back neck row ends, and knit up sts from left front invisible casting on.
1st and 2nd rows: Using C6, K.
3rd row: Using C4, K.
4th and 5th rows: Using C6, K.

Using M1, work 6 rows in moss st.
Next row: Work 14 sts in moss st, cast off 3 sts for buttonhole. Work another 2 buttonholes at regular intervals on unshaped edge of front (see Placing Buttonholes, page 14).

Work another 6 rows in moss stitch, casting on 3 sts over each buttonhole in next row.

Cast off in moss stitch.

Making up

Darn in loose ends. Sew on buttons. Do not press.

Sideways-knitted Jacket or Sweater

First make a tension sample (see on page 10) and take measurements (see on page 11).

Right sleeve

Using a set of four double-pointed needles or a short circular needle, begin at the end of the right sleeve.

Long sleeve: From your stitch tension, calculate the number of sts required for the wrist. Cast on this number of sts and work the wristband in rib or your choice of stitch.

Next calculate number of sts required for the upper arm. Subtract the wrist sts from this number to obtain the number of sts to increase.

From your row tension, calculate the number of rows in the sleeve length minus 5 cm. Divide the number of sleeve increases by 2 to obtain the number of increasing rows, then divide the calculated number of sleeve rows by this number to obtain the number of rounds between each increase. This number should be 4 or 6. To make it easier to obtain this result, a few sts can be increased in the first row above the cuff.

Increase 1 st at the beginning and end of each increasing round until you have the required number of sts for the upper arm, then work 5 cm without shaping.

Short sleeve: Decide how wide you want the sleeve to be then cast on the required number of sts for the desired width of the lower edge of the sleeve. Work with or without shaping as required until sleeve is the desired length.

Right side of front and back

Calculate the number of sts required for the length desired from the underarm to the lower edge. Transfer sleeve sts to a circular needle. Using the same yarn, invisibly cast on this number of sts.

Work back across the cast-on sts, work half the sleeve sts, place a marker and work the rest of the sleeve sts then knit up the calculated number of underarm sts from the invisible casting on.

Work in rows on these sts until the body measures the length required for the shoulder measurement, ending with a wrong-side row.

Right front

First decide the depth of the V shaping. Mark this point on the front.

From your row tension, calculate the number of rows required for the back neck measurement (usually one-third of the shoulder measurement). You will need half this number of rows for your neck shaping.

Divide the number of rows in the neck shaping by 2 to obtain the number of steps in the shaping. Then divide the number of sts in the shaped edge by the number of steps to obtain the number of sts in each step. If the number does not divide evenly, make up the difference on the last step.

Work the shaping in short rows. Work to the calculated number of sts in the steps before the marker, turn and work to end of row. Continue in this manner until you have reached the bottom of the V, then work all the front sts to the end of the row at the back. Thread the front sts onto a length of left-over yarn.

Centre back

Work back to the marker, then work the required number of rows for the back neck measurement, ending with a wrong-side row (neck end).

Left front

Sweater   Invisibly cast on the required number of sts for the V-neck shaping, then work the sts for the unshaped edge of the right front.

Jacket   Invisibly cast on the number of sts for the whole front.

Work the neck shaping to correspond with the right front, ending with a wrong-side row.

Left side of front and back

Work across front and back until left shoulder corresponds with right shoulder.

Left sleeve

Slip onto an extra needle the same number of sts as you cast on for the right underarm. Hold these sts alongside the back sts and join them together either by grafting or by one of the methods described in the Joining Shoulders section on page 12.

Distribute the rest of the sts on three double-pointed needles and complete the sleeve to correspond with the right sleeve, decreasing instead of increasing for shaping.

Basque

This may be done in one of two ways. It may be worked at the same time as the body of the garment by working the first and last few sts in the row in a different stitch pattern (e.g. moss stitch).

If you wish to have a separate ribbed basque, make the body about 5 cm shorter than the desired length. Using a circular needle two sizes smaller than the main needle, pick up 1 st for every row around the bottom edge and work in rib for 5 cm or desired length. If you are using K 2, P 2 rib for a sweater, be sure that the number of sts on the needle is divisible by 4. Cast off loosely in rib.

Sweater neckband

Using a smaller sized circular needle, pick up 1 st for every row along back neck, knit up the sts from the invisible casting on on the left side of neck, then knit up the sts from the length of yarn on the right side.

Work in rib until the band is the desired width and cast off loosely in rib.

Jacket front band

Beginning at the bottom edge of the right front, work the sts from the length of yarn, pick up 1 st for each row across the back neck then knit up sts from invisible casting on on left front.

Work the band in rib or your chosen stitch pattern, working buttonholes in the middle row on right front.

Making up

Darn in ends. Sew buttons on jacket. Press if desired.

Raglan School Sweater in 8-ply

Illustrated on page 47

A seamless sweater, worked from the top down, in classic raglan style to go with any school uniform.

Fits chest size (cm)

A	B	C	D	E	F	G	H
55	60	**65**	70	**75**	80	**85**	90

Measures (cm)

60	66	**75**	80	**85**	90	**95**	100

Sleeve length, underarm to wrist (cm)

24	28	**30**	34	**39**	42	**44**	45

Materials

50gm balls of 8-ply yarn
5: 6: **7**: 8: **10**: 12: **13**: 13 balls
Circular needles and sets of four double-pointed needles in sizes 4 mm and 3.25 mm. For sizes A, B, C and D, use 60 cm circular needles; for all other sizes use 80 cm.
Small quantity of left-over yarn
Stitch-holder

Tension

22 sts and 30 rows to 10 cm, measured over st-st using 4 mm needles.

INSTRUCTIONS

The work begins at the neck by casting on sts for the back of the neck and the top of the sleeves.

Using 4 mm circular needle, invisibly cast on **34**: 42: **40**: 44: **50**: 50: **56**: 56 sts.
1st row: P 2, PM, P **6**: 8: **7**: 8: **10**: 9: **11**: 10, PM, P **18**: 22: **22**: 24: **26**: 28: **30**: 32, PM, P **6**: 8: 7: 8: **10**: 9: **11**: 10, PM, P 2.
2nd row: K to 1 st before marker, inc 1, K 1, *SM, K 1, inc 1, K to 1 st before next marker, inc 1, K 1*, rep from * to * twice, SM, K 1, inc 1, K end.
3rd row: **Sizes B and C:** P. **Other sizes:** P to marker, *SM, P 1, inc 1 P, P to 1 st before marker, inc 1 P, P 1*, SM, P to next marker, rep from * to *, SM, P to end.
4th row: As 2nd row.
Rep 3rd and 4th rows **1**: 0: **0**: 3: **3**: 8: **7**: 8 times.
Next and alternate rows: P.
The increases on either side of the markers form the raglan lines which divide the sleeves from the body. Continue in this manner, increasing every alternate row as in 2nd row on either side of each marker at raglan lines until **19**: 15: **23**: 23: **21**: 21: **21**: 21 rows have been completed from the beginning.
Next row: K 1, inc 1, *K to 1 st before marker, inc 1, K 1, SM, K 1, inc 1*, rep from * to * 3 times, K to last st, inc 1, K 1.
The increases at the beginning and end of this row begin the shaping for the neck. Continue in this manner, increasing at raglan lines in every alternate row, while at the same time increasing at neck edge every 4th row until **47**: 51: **59**: 63: **65**: 69: **73**: 77 rows have been completed from the beginning.
This brings the garment to the level of the underarms.
Break off yarn and slip left front sts (to 1st marker) onto right-hand needle point.

Left sleeve

**Change to 4 mm double-pointed needles and knit sleeve sts to 2nd marker, dividing sts onto 3 needles.

Invisibly cast on **2**: 2: **3**: 2: **4**: 3: **3**: 2 sts, placing half the cast-on sts on the first double-pointed needle and half on the third (**58**: 60: **68**: 80: **86**: 98: **102**: 106 sts).

Thread remaining sts on the circular needle onto a length of left-over yarn, taking care to keep the markers in place.

Continue working on the double-pointed needles in rounds until sleeve measures 5 cm.

Next round: K 1, K 2 tog, work to last 3 sts, sl 1, K 1, psso, K 1. Decrease in this manner every **4th**: 6th: **6th**: 4th: **4th**: 4th: **4th**: 4th round until **36**: 42: **48**: 44: **42**: 50: **50**: 52 sts remain.

Work **3**: 5: **5**: 3: **3**: 3: **3**: 3 rounds without shaping.

Next round: Decrease **0**: 2: **8**: 2: **0**: 6: **4**: 4 sts evenly over round (**36**: 40: **40**: 42: **42**: 44: **46**: 48 sts).

Change to 3.25 mm double-pointed needles and work in K 1, P 1 rib for 5 cm. Cast off loosely in rib.**

Right sleeve

Using 4 mm circular needle, join in yarn at left-front end of underarm casting on. Knit across cast-on sts. Knit the sts from the length of yarn across back to next marker. Rep from ** to **.

Body

Using the 4 mm circular needle, join in yarn at right-back end of underarm casting on. Knit across half the cast-on sts, PM, knit the rest of the cast-on sts. Knit up the rest of the sts from the length of yarn (right front) and join into a round by knitting onto the left front sts from the length of yarn (**132**: 148: **166**: 176: **188**: 198: **210**: 220 sts).

Continue working in rounds, keeping the marker in place, until the body is desired length minus 5 cm. Beginning at the marker, change to 3.25 mm circular needle and work in K 1, P 1 rib for 5 cm. Cast off loosely in rib.

Neckband

Using 3.25 mm double-pointed needles, with right side of work facing, join in yarn at right-hand end of invisibly cast-on sts and K **34**: 42: **40**: 44: **50**: 50: **56**: 56 sts. Pick up **36**: 38: **44**: 48: **50**: 52: **56**: 58 sts evenly along left front, PM, pick up 1 st from centre of V, then **35**: 37: **43**: 47: **49**: 51: **55**: 57 sts along right front (**90**: 98: **110**: 120: **126**: 132: **142**: 148 sts). Divide sts evenly onto 3 needles.

1st round: (K 1, P 1) to end.

2nd round: (K 1, P 1) to 2 sts before marker, sl 1, K 1, psso, K 1, K 2 tog, P 1, (K 1, P 1) to end.

3rd round: (K 1, P 1) to 2 sts before marker, P 2 tog, K 1, P 2 tog, (K 1, P 1) to end.

Rep 2nd and 3rd rounds 3 times. Cast off loosely in rib.

Making up

Darn in loose ends. Press if desired.

Raglan School Sweater in 5-ply

Illustrated on page 47

A lighter-weight version of the previous pattern.

Fits chest size (cm)

A	B	C	D	E	F	G	H
55	60	**65**	70	**75**	80	**85**	90

Measures (cm)

60	66	**75**	80	**85**	90	**95**	100

Sleeve length, underarm to wrist (cm)

24	28	**30**	34	**39**	42	**44**	45

Materials

50 gm balls of 5-ply yarn
4: 5: **6**: 8: **9**: 10: **11**: 12 balls
Circular needles and sets of four double-pointed needles in sizes 3.75 mm and 3 mm. For sizes A, B, C and D, use 60 cm circular needles; for all other sizes use 80 cm.
Small quantity of left-over yarn
Stitch-holder

Tension

26 sts and 36 rows to 10 cm, measured over st-st, using 3.75 mm needles.

INSTRUCTIONS

The work begins at the neck by casting on sts for the back of the neck and the top of the sleeves.

Using 3.75 mm circular needle, invisibly cast on **42**: 44: **50**: 52: **54**: 62: **64**: 66 sts.
1st row: P 2, PM, P **8**: 8: **10**: 10: **10**: 12: **12**: 12, PM,
P **22**: 24: **26**: 28: **30**: 34: **36**: 38, PM, P **8**: 8: **10**: 10: **10**: 12: **12**: 12, PM, P 2.
2nd row: K to 1 st before marker, K 1, inc 1, *SM, K 1, inc 1, K to 1 st before next marker, inc 1, K 1*, rep from * to * twice, SM, K 1, inc 1, K to end.
3rd row: **Sizes B and C:** P. **Other sizes:** P to marker, *SM, P 1, inc 1 P, P to 1 st before marker, inc 1 P, P 1*, SM, P to next marker, rep from * to *, SM, P to end.
4th row: As 2nd row.

Rep 3rd and 4th rows **1**: 0: **0**: 3: **5**: 8: **9**: 10 times.
Next and alternate rows: P.

The increases on either side of the markers form the raglan lines which divide the sleeves from the body. Continue in this manner, increasing every alternate row as in 2nd row on either side of each marker at raglan lines until **19**: 21: **27**: 27: **27**: 23: **23**: 23 rows have been completed from the beginning.

Next row: K 1, inc 1, *K to 1 st before marker, inc 1, K 1, SM, K 1, inc 1*, rep from * to * 3 times, K to last st, inc 1, K 1.

The increases at the beginning and end of this row begin the shaping for the neck. Continue in this manner, increasing at raglan lines in every alternate row, while at the same time increasing at neck edge every 4th row until **55**: 61: **71**: 75: **79**: 83: **87**: 91 rows have been completed from the beginning.

This brings the garment to the level of the underarms.

Break off yarn and slip left-front sts (to 1st marker) onto right-hand needle point.

Left sleeve

**Change to 3.75 mm double-pointed needles and knit sleeve sts to 2nd marker, dividing sts onto 3 needles.

Invisibly cast on **2**: 2: **2**: 2: **3**: 2: **2**: 2 sts, placing half the cast-on sts on the first double-pointed

69

needle and half on the third (**68**: 70: **82**: 94: **102**: 114: **120**: 126 sts).

Thread remaining sts on the circular needle onto a length of left-over yarn, taking care to keep the markers in place.

Continue working on the double-pointed needles in rounds until sleeve measures 5 cm.
Next round: K 1, K 2 tog, work to last 3 sts, sl 1, K 1, psso, K 1. Decrease in this manner every **4th**: 6th: **6th**: 4th: **4th**: 4th: **4th**: 4th round until **42**: 48: **58**: 50: **50**: 56: **58**: 62 sts remain.

Work **3**: 5: **5**: 3: **3**: 3: **3**: 3 rounds without shaping.
Next round: Decrease **0**: 2: **10**: 0: **0**: 4: **2**: 4 sts evenly over round (**42**: 46: **48**: 50: **50**: 52: **56**: 58 sts).

Change to 3 mm double-pointed needles and work in K 1, P 1 rib for 5 cm. Cast off loosely in rib.**

Right sleeve

Using 3.75 mm circular needle, join in yarn at left-front end of underarm casting on. Knit across cast-on sts. Knit the sts from the length of yarn across back to next marker. Rep from ** to **.

Body

Using 3.75 mm circular needle, join in yarn at right-back end of underarm casting on. Knit across half the cast-on sts, PM, knit the rest of the cast-on sts. Knit up the rest of the sts from the length of yarn (right front) and join into a round by knitting onto the left front sts from the length of yarn (**156**: 172: **196**: 208: **220**: 236: **248**: 260 sts).

Continue working in rounds, keeping the marker in place, until the body is desired length minus 5 cm. Beginning at the marker, change to 3 mm circular needle and work in K 1, P 1 rib for 5 cm. Cast off loosely in rib.

Neckband

Using 3 mm double-pointed needles, with right side of work facing, join in yarn at right-hand end of invisibly cast-on sts and K **42**: 44: **50**: 52: **54**: 62: **64**: 66 sts. Pick up **42**: 46: **54**: 56: **60**: 62: **66**: 68 sts evenly along left front, PM, pick up 1 st from centre of V, then **41**: 45: **53**: 55: **59**: 61: **65**: 67 sts along right front (**126**: 136: **158**: 164: **174**: 186: **196**: 202 sts). Divide sts evenly onto 3 needles.
1st round: (K 1, P 1) to end.
2nd round: (K 1, P 1) to 2 sts before marker, sl 1, K 1, psso, K 1, K 2 tog, P 1, (K 1, P 1) to end.
3rd round: (K 1, P 1) to 2 sts before marker, P 2 tog, K 1, P 2 tog, (K 1, P 1) to end.

Rep 2nd and 3rd rounds 3 times. Cast off loosely in rib.

Making up

Darn in loose ends. Press if desired.

Raglan Dress

Illustrated on page 58

This dress, worked in 8-ply yarn on larger needles, features a geometric design on the body and sleeves in three contrasting colours. The neck, sleeves and hem are finished in moss stitch.

Fits chest size (cm)

A	B	C	D
85	90	**95**	100

Measures (cm)

95	100	**105**	110

Sleeve length, underarm to wrist (cm)

44	45	**47**	48

Materials

50 gm balls of 8-ply yarn
Main colour: **13**: 14: **15**: 17 balls
Contrasting colours: C1, 2 balls; C2 and C3, 1 ball each
3 buttons
80 cm circular needles and set of four double-pointed needles in size 5 mm

Tension

19 sts and 26 rows to 10 cm, measured over st-st, using 5 mm needles.

INSTRUCTIONS

The work begins at the neck by casting on sts for the neck and the top of the sleeves.

Using circular needle, cast on **91**: 95: **95**: 97 sts.

Work the first 8 rows in moss stitch as follows: 1st row: (K 1, P 1) to end. 2nd and following rows: K the P sts and P the K sts as they present.
1st row: Work 19, PM, work **12**: 14: **14**: 15, PM, work 30, PM, work **12**: 14: **14**: 15, PM, work 18.
2nd row: Work to 1 st before marker, inc 1, K 1, *SM, K 1, inc 1, work to 1 st before next marker, inc 1, K 1,* rep from * to * twice, SM, K 1, inc 1, work to end.
3rd row: Work to marker, *SM, work to next marker,* rep from * to * twice, SM, work to last 5 sts, cast off 2 sts for buttonhole, work 3.
4th row: As 2nd row, casting on 2 sts for buttonhole.

The increases on either side of the markers form the raglan lines which divide the sleeves from the body. Continue in this manner, increasing every alternate row as in 2nd row on either side of each marker at raglan lines. After 8 rows have been completed in moss stitch, continue working in st-st, working the first and last 7 sts of each row in moss stitch, until 50 rows have been completed from the beginning, working two more buttonholes as before in the 23rd and 24th and 43rd and 44th rows.

51st row: Continuing increases as before, work to last 7 sts. Place these 7 sts onto a separate needle and hold them in front of the last 7 sts so that the right side moss-stitch band overlaps the left. K tog the sts on the front and back needle, then continue working in rounds, working the increases at the raglan line as before, until **55**: 55: **55**: 61 rows and rounds have been completed from the beginning.

Continue the raglan increases as follows:
**1st round:* Inc on body sides only of raglan line.
2nd and 4th rounds: K.
3rd round: Inc on body and sleeve sides of raglan line.*

Rep from * to * **1**: 2: **3**: 4 times, then 1st round once.
Next round: K.

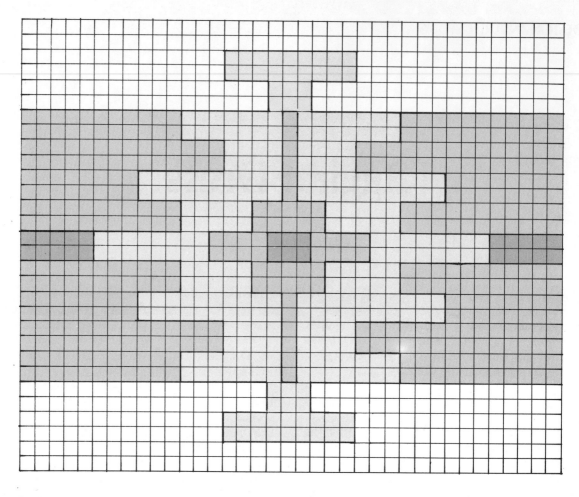

Graph of pattern for body of raglan dress

This brings the garment to the level of the underarm. The next step is to work the sleeves.

Left sleeve

**Change to double-pointed needles and knit sleeve sts to 2nd marker, dividing sts onto 3 needles.

Invisibly cast on **2**: **2**: **2**: 3 sts, placing half the cast-on sts on the first double-pointed needle and half on the third (**70**: 74: **76**: 80 sts).

Thread remaining sts on the circular needle onto a length of left-over yarn, taking care to keep the markers in place.

Continue working on the double-pointed needles in rounds until sleeve measures 5 cm, at the same time commencing the pattern as shown in the graph.

Next round: K 1, K 2 tog, K **27**: 28: **29**: 32, K 9 in C1, work to last 3 sts, sl 1, K 1, psso, K 1. Continue pattern from graph, decreasing in this manner every 6th round until **40**: 42: **44**: 46 sts remain.

Work 5 rounds without shaping.

Work 12 rounds in moss stitch. Cast off loosely in moss stitch.**

Right sleeve

Using circular needle, join in yarn at left-front end of underarm casting on. Knit across cast-on sts. Knit the sts from the length of yarn across back to next marker. Rep from ** to **.

Body

Using circular needle, join in yarn at right-back end of underarm casting on. Knit across half the cast-on sts, PM, knit the rest of the cast-on sts. Knit up the rest of the sts from the length of yarn (**184**: 192: **200**: 210 sts).

Continue working in rounds, keeping the marker in place.

1st round: *K **42**: 43: **46**: 48, K 9 in C1, K **41**: 44: **45**: 48*, rep from * to *.

Continue working the pattern from the graph, then work in main colour until the body is desired length minus 4 cm. Beginning at the marker, work 12 rounds in moss stitch. Cast off loosely in moss stitch.

Making up:

Darn in loose ends. Sew on buttons. Press if desired.

Raglan Sweater

First make a tension sample (see page 10) and take measurements (see page 11). The shoulder measurement will not be used in the usual way for this design, but will be needed to calculate the sleeve-top sts and may be taken as a guide for the back neck measurement, which should be one-third of the shoulder measurement. One extra measurement will need to be taken for this design, and that is the raglan depth. Measure this from the point where the raglan line is to begin at the neck to the underarm.

Begin by calculating the number of sts to cast on. From the stitch tension calculate the number of sts required for the back neck measurement. Next calculate the number of sts required for the sleeve tops by calculating the number of sts which would be required for the shoulder measurement and dividing the result by 9.

Using a circular needle, cast on the back neck sts plus twice the number of sleeve-top sts plus 4. Work the first row as follows (wrong side): P 2, PM, P sleeve-top sts, PM, P back neck sts, PM, P sleeve-top sts, PM, P 2.

The markers mark the position of the increases which will form the raglan lines. Work the next and following alternate rows as follows: K to 1 st before marker, inc 1, K 1, *SM, K 1, inc 1, K to 1 st before next marker, inc 1, K 1*, rep from * to * twice, SM, K 1, inc 1, K to end.

These increases form the raglan line which separates the body from the sleeves.

Before going any further some more calculations must be made. First calculate the number of sts required for the chest measurement and for the upper arm measurement. Next use your row tension to calculate the number of rows which will be needed for the raglan depth measurement.

The next step is to calculate the number of sts to be cast on at the underarm. To do this, add the number of sts in the back neck to the number of rows in the raglan line and subtract one. Subtract the result from the number of sts in the chest measurement. This will give the number of underarm cast ons.

The next step is to check whether the increases on the raglan lines will give you the correct number of sts for the upper arm and the chest. First check the upper arm. As there are two increases in every alternate row on each sleeve section, you will be adding the equivalent of one st for every row in the raglan line. Add together the number of rows in the raglan line, the number of sleeve-top sts cast on at the beginning of the work and the number of sts which you have calculated for the underarm casting on. If the result is larger than the required number of sts for the upper arm, adjust this by increasing on the body sides only of the raglan line, omitting the sleeve-side increases, in the rows before the underarm. If there will not be enough sts in the upper arm, increase in every row at the top of the sleeve until you have added sufficient sts to make up the difference.

To check the chest sts, add together two sts for each row in the raglan line, plus twice the number of back neck sts, plus twice the number of underarm cast ons. Check the result against the required number of sts for the chest. If it is more or less than the required number, adjust the increases in the same way as for the sleeve.

Neck shaping

V-neck: Increase at neck edge every 4th row until half the number of back neck sts have been added on each side. The increases should finish 3 rows above the underarm. Use the number of rows in the raglan line to calculate the row where the increases should begin: Divide the number of rows by 4, then multiply the number of sts to be increased on each side by 4. Subtract the second number from the first. The result will give you the number of the row on which to begin the neck increases. When the neck increases are finished, work 3 more rows then join the work together and work in rounds.

Crew neck: Work without shaping at neck edge for approximately 2.5 cm. Increase every alternate row at neck edge until you have added one-quarter of the number of back neck sts on each side. Work 1 row, then invisibly cast on half the number of back neck sts. Join work together and work in rounds.

Sleeves

When the required number of rows have been worked for the raglan depth, break off yarn and slip sts to 1st marker onto right-hand needle point. Change to double-pointed needles and work sleeve to 2nd marker, dividing sts onto 3 needles. Invisibly cast on the calculated number of sts for the underarm, placing half the cast-on sts on the first double-pointed needle and half on the third.

Thread the remaining sts on the circular needle onto a length of left-over yarn, taking care to keep the markers in place. Work in rounds until the sleeve measures 5 cm, then decrease at each end of every 4th or 6th round until the sleeve is the required length minus 5 cm.

To work out the decreasing intervals required to make the sleeve the correct length, first calculate the number of rows in the shaped part of the sleeve (sleeve length minus 10 cm). Subtract the wrist sts from the upper arm sts and divide the result by 2. This will give you the number of decreasing rows. Divide the calculated number of rows in the shaped part of the sleeve first by 4 and then by 6. Choose whichever result is closest to the number of wrist sts but not less than that number. On the last round, decrease any excess sts evenly over the round so that the final number is equal to the number of sts required for the wrist.

Change to smaller sized double-pointed needles and work 5 cm in rib.

Join in yarn at left-front end of underarm casting on, work across cast-on sts then work across back to next marker. Work another sleeve to correspond.

Body

Join in yarn at right-back end of underarm casting on. Work across the cast-on sts then work the front sts. Continue working in rounds until the body is the desired length minus 5 cm.

Change to smaller sized circular needle and work in rib for 5 cm. If you wish to work the band in K 2, P 2 rib, make sure that the number of sts is divisible by 4. If it is not, decrease the appropriate number of sts evenly over the last round before the ribbing.

Neckband

V-neck: Using smaller sized double-pointed needles, join in yarn at right-hand end and knit up invisibly cast-on sts. Pick up 3 sts for every 4 rows down left side. If you are going to work the band in K 1, P 1 rib, place a marker at this point then pick up 1 st from the centre of the V. If you are going to work the band in K 2, P 2 rib, first make sure that the number of sts is divisible by 4, then place a marker before the last 2 sts picked up on the side (centre of V). In order to ensure that these 2 centre sts are knit sts, it may be necessary to begin the rounds with P 2 instead of K 2. Pick up the same number of sts on the right side and divide the sts onto 3 needles. Work in rib until the band is desired width, decreasing before and after the marker in every round if working in K 1, P 1 rib. If working in K 2, P 2 rib, work the decreases before the marker, then K 2 and decrease again. Cast off loosely in rib.

Crew neck: Using smaller sized double-pointed needles, join in yarn at right-hand end and knit up invisibly cast-on sts. Pick up 3 sts for every 4 rows down left side, then knit up sts from invisible casting on and pick up the same number of sts on the right side. Divide sts evenly onto 3 needles. If you are going to work the band in K 2, P 2 rib, make sure that the number of sts is divisible by 4. Work in rib until the band is desired width. Cast off loosely in rib.

Making up

Darn in loose ends. Press if desired.

Lace-trimmed short-sleeved top (page 81); the picture below shows detail of the lace trim

Short-sleeved cotton top (facing page)

Cotton Top

Illustrated on facing page

This cool short-sleeved cotton top features a wide neckline with a check stitch pattern around the edges and down the sides of the back and front.

Fits chest size (cm)

A	B	C	D	E	F	G
60	65	**70**	75	**80**	85	**90**

Measures (cm)

66	75	**80**	85	**90**	95	**100**

Materials

50 gm balls of 4-ply cotton yarn
4: 4: **4**: 4: **5**: 5: **5** balls
Circular needles and 2 sets of four double-pointed needles in size 3.25 mm. For sizes A, B, C and D use 60 cm circular needles; for all other sizes use 80 cm.
2 stitch-holders

Tension

27 sts and 34 rows to 10 cm, measured over stocking stitch.

Check stitch

1st round: (K 2, P 2) to end.
2nd and 3rd rounds: K the K sts and P the P sts as they present.
4th round: P the K sts and K the P sts as they present.
5th and 6th rounds: As 2nd round.

INSTRUCTIONS

The work begins at the bottom edge. Using the thumb method, cast on **180**: 200: **216**: 228: **244**: 256: **268** sts, placing a marker at the end of the round.
Work 12 rounds in check st.
Next round: *Work 10 sts in check st, K **62**: 72: **78**: 84: **90**: 96: **102**, work 10 sts in check st, K **8**: 8: **10**: 10: **12**: 12: **12***, rep from * to *.
Rep this round until the body is the desired length to armhole.

Back

1st row: Work 10 sts in check st, K **62**: 72: **78**: 84: **90**: 96: **102**, work 10 sts in check st, turn.
2nd row: Work 10 sts in check st, P **62**: 72: **78**: 84: **90**: 96: **102**, work 10 sts in check st.
Work **38**: 44: **48**: 52: **58**: 62: **68** more rows, keeping check st pattern correct.
1st row: Work 10 sts in check st, K **3**: 6: **7**: 9: **11**: 13: **14**, work **56**: 60: **64**: 66: **68**: 70: **74** sts in check st, K **3**: 6: **7**: 9: **11**: 13: **14**, work 10 sts in check st.
2nd row: Work 10 sts in check st, P **3**: 6: **7**: 9: **11**: 13: **14**, work **56**: 60: **64**: 66: **68**: 70: **74** sts in check st, P **3**: 6: **7**: 9: **11**: 13: **14**, work 10 sts in check st.
Rep these 2 rows 5 times.
Next row: *Work 10 sts in check st, K **3**: 6: **7**: 9: **11**: 13: **14**, work 10 sts in check st*, cast off **36**: 40: **44**: 46: **48**: 50: **54**, rep from * to *.
Break off yarn and place shoulder sts onto double-pointed needles.

Front

Place **8**: 8: **10**: 10: **12**: 12: **12** sts from left side underarm on a stitch-holder. Join in yarn and work across front, keeping check st pattern correct. Place last **8**: 8: **10**: 10: **12**: 12: **12** sts from right-side underarm on a stitch-holder. Work **8**: 12: **12**: 14: **18**: 18: **22** rows as for back.

1st row: Work 10 sts in check st, K **12**: 16: **18**: 21: **23**: 25: **27**, work **38**: 40: **42**: 42: **44**: 46: **48** sts in check st, K **12**: 16: **18**: 21: **23**: 25: **27**, work 10 sts in check st.

2nd row: Work 10 sts in check st, P **12**: 16: **18**: 21: **23**: 25: **27**, work **38**: 40: **42**: 42: **44**: 46: **48** sts in check st, P **12**: 16: **18**: 21: **23**: 25: **27**, work 10 sts in check st.

Rep these 2 rows 5 times.

Shape neck

Next row: Work 10 sts in check st, K **12**: 16: **18**: 21: **23**: 25: **27**, work 10 sts in check st, turn.

Work left side of front on these sts.

1st row: Work 10 sts in check st, P **12**: 16: **18**: 21: **23**: 25: **27**, work 10 sts in check st.

2nd row: Work 10 sts in check st, K **10**: 14: **16**: 19: **21**: 23: **25**, sl 1, K 1, psso, work 10 sts in check st.

Continue in this manner, decreasing 1 st before check st pattern at neck edge every alternate row **8**: 9: **10**: 10: **11**: 12: **13** more times.

Work **4**: 4: **6**: 8: **8**: 10: **10** more rows without shaping. Break off yarn and place sts onto a double-pointed needle.

Join in yarn to centre front and cast off **18**: 20: **22**: 22: **24**: 26: **28** sts.

Complete right front to correspond with left front, working decreases as K 2 tog.

Left shoulder saddle and sleeve

Using the thumb method, cast on 8 sts onto the neck end of the double-pointed needle holding the left back shoulder sts.

1st row: Slip the 1st st on the left front shoulder onto the left-hand needle point. Work 10 sts in check st, turn.

2nd row: Work 1 st from back shoulder tog with 1st saddle st, work in check st to last saddle st, work last st together with 1 st at neck end of front shoulder sts.

3rd row: Work 1 st from front shoulder tog with 1st saddle st, work in check st to last saddle st, work last st together with 1 st at neck end of back shoulder sts.

4th row: Work to end (do not work sts together).*

Rep from * to * until all the sts on the back and front shoulders have been taken up. Break off yarn.

Rejoin yarn at lower edge of left front armhole and pick up **34**: 38: **42**: 44: **48**: 50: **54** sts evenly along armhole edge. Work across shoulder saddle sts then pick up **34**: 38: **42**: 44: **48**: 50: **54** sts evenly along right armhole edge. K **8**: 8: **10**: 10: **12**: 12: **12** sts from underarm stitch-holder. Distribute the sts evenly onto 3 needles, placing half the underarm sts on the first needle and half on the third (**86**: 94: **104**: 108: **118**: 122: **130** sts).

1st round: K **3**: 3: **4**: 4: **5**: 5: **5**, K 2 tog, K **33**: 37: **41**: 43: **47**: 49: **53**, work 10 sts in check st, K **33**: 37: **41**: 43: **47**: 49: **53**, sl 1, K 1, psso, K **3**: 3: **4**: 4: **5**: 5: **5**.

2nd round: K **37**: 40: **46**: 48: **53**: 55: **59**, work 10 sts in check st, K **37**: 40: **46**: 48: **53**: 55: **59**.

3rd round: K **2**: 2: **3**: 3: **4**: 4: **4**, K 2 tog, K **32**: 36: **40**: 42: **46**: 48: **53**, work 10 sts in check st, K **32**: 36: **40**: 42: **46**: 48: **53**, sl 1, K 1, psso, K **2**: 2: **3**: 3: **4**: 4: **4**.

Continue in this manner, working together 1 st from underarm with 1 st from sleeve at each end on every alternate round until 2 underarm sts are left (**80**: 88: **96**: 100: **108**: 112: **120** sts).

Work 6 cm without shaping.

Work 12 rounds in check st then cast off loosely in check st.

Work right shoulder saddle and sleeve to correspond.

Making up

Darn in ends. Press if desired.

Cotton Top

First make a tension sample (see page 10) and take measurements (see page 11).

Choose a stitch pattern for the edges of the body, sleeves and neckline and for the panels on the front and back and the shoulder saddle. This should be a simple pattern such as moss stitch, double moss or basket stitch.

From your tension sample calculate the number of sts required for the chest measurement. Adjust this number so that it is a multiple of the number of sts in the stitch pattern. For example, if you are using K 2, P 2 check stitch the number of stitches must be divisible by four.

Using a circular needle, cast on this number of sts by the thumb method and work in your chosen stitch pattern until the edge is desired depth.

Next calculate the number of sts required for the shoulder measurement. Decide how many sts you would like to have in your chosen stitch pattern in the panel on each side of the body. Subtract twice this number from the number of shoulder sts. This will give you the number of sts to be worked in stocking stitch between the two panels.

Next calculate the number of underarm sts by subtracting twice the number of shoulder sts from the chest sts and dividing the result by 2.

On the next round, work as follows: *pattern sts, calculated number of stocking stitch sts, pattern sts, underarm sts*, rep from * to *.

Continue working in this manner until the body is the desired length to underarm.

Back

First calculate the depth of the armhole. Calculate the number of sts required for the sleeve measurement and subtract from it the number of sts which will be in the shoulder saddle. Divide this number by 2, then convert sts into rows by dividing

the result by 2 and multiplying by 3. This will give the number of rows to be worked for the armhole.

Work the calculated number of rows minus the number of rows you wish to have in your chosen stitch pattern for the neck edge.

Next calculate the number of back neck sts. The back neck is usually one-third of the shoulder measurement, but you may wish to make it wider for this design. Add the number of sts required for the stitch pattern on either side of the neck then subtract this number from the shoulder sts. Divide the result by 2. On the next row work this number of sts, then work the calculated number of pattern sts and work to end of row.

Continue in this manner until the neck edging is the desired width. On the last row, cast off the calculated number of back neck sts, break off yarn and leave the shoulder sts on double-pointed needles.

Front

Leave underarm sts on stitch-holders and work as for back until you reach the desired neck depth, minus the required number of rows for your stitch pattern edging.

Next calculate the number of sts to cast off for the centre front neck edge. This is normally half the number of back neck sts but you may make it wider if you wish.

Subtract the front neck cast-offs from the shoulder sts and divide the result by 2. For the left front, work this number of sts, working in stitch pattern at neck edge.

To shape neck, decrease 1 st at neck edge of every alternate row before the stitch pattern, until you have taken off half the number of centre front cast-offs, then work without shaping until the front measures the same as the back. Leave the sts on a double-pointed needle.

Cast off the required number of sts for the centre front and complete the right front to correspond with the back.

Shoulder saddle and sleeve

Using the thumb method, cast on 2 less than the desired number of sts for the shoulder saddle and work in your chosen stitch pattern. Work the first row, taking the last st at the neck end of the front shoulder sts for the first saddle st, and the first st at the neck end of the back shoulder sts for the last saddle st.

At the beginning and the end of the second and third rows, work the first and last st together with 1 st from the back and front shoulders. Work the fourth row without working these sts together. Continue in this manner, taking up 1 st from the back and front shoulders in 2 rows out of every 3 until all the sts from the back and front shoulders are taken up.

Break off yarn and rejoin it at the lower edge of the armhole. Using double-pointed needles, pick up sleeve sts along edge of armhole. The number of sts to be picked up will be the calculated number of sleeve sts minus the number of shoulder saddle sts divided by 2. Work across the saddle sts then pick up the same number of sts along other edge of armhole and work underarm sts from stitch-holder.

Work in rounds, continuing stitch pattern from shoulder saddle and working together 1 st from underarm and 1 st from sleeve at each end of every alternate round until 2 underarm sts remain, then work without shaping until sleeve is desired length minus stitch pattern edging.

Work edging in stitch pattern and cast off loosely.

Work other shoulder saddle and sleeve to correspond.

Making up

Darn in ends. Press if desired.

PATTERN

Lace-trimmed Short-sleeved Top

Illustrated on page 75

This lightweight top features a picot-edged neckline and short set sleeves. It has a band of lace pattern around the lower edge which is finished with a narrow lace edging. The same lace edging is used to finish the sleeves.

Fits chest size (cm)

A	B	C	D	E
80	85	**90**	95	**100**

Measures (cm)

90	93	**100**	103.5	**107**

Materials

50 gm balls of 4-ply yarn
7: 7: **7**: 7: **8** balls
60 cm and 80 cm circular needles and a set of four double-pointed needles in size 3.25 mm
Small quantity of left-over yarn

Tension

28 sts and 36 rows to 10 cm, measured over stocking stitch, using 3.25 mm needles.

INSTRUCTIONS

Begin the work at the back shoulder. Start with the 60 cm circular needle and change to the 80 cm needle when there are enough sts to fit on it.
Invisibly cast on **96**: 96: **102**: 102: **104** sts.
1st row: P.
2nd row: K **80**: 80: **84**: 84: **86**, turn.

3rd row: P **64**: 64: **66**: 66: **68**, turn.
4th row: K **72**: 72: **75**: 75: **77**, turn.
5th row: P **80**: 80: **84**: 84: **86**, turn.
6th row: K to end.
7th row: P.
    Work **14**: 16: **18**: 18: **18** more rows in st-st. Break off yarn, leave sts on circular needle.

Front shoulders

With right side of work facing and using the right-hand end of circular needle, pick up and knit **24**: 24: **26**: 26: **26** sts from invisible cast-on (right front). Using a second ball of yarn, miss **48**: 48: **50**: 50: **52** sts, join in yarn and knit up **24**: 24: **26**: 26: **26** sts (left front).
1st row: P across left and right fronts.
2nd row: K back across right front, K 8 on left front.
3rd row: P back across left front, P 8 on right front.
4th row: K back across right front, K **16**: 16: **18**: 18: **18** on left front.
5th row: P back across left front, P **16**: 16: **18**: 18: **18** on right front.
6th row: K back across right front, K to end of left front.
7th row: P across left front, P to end of right front.
    Working across both right and left front, work **14**: 16: **18**: 18: **18** more rows in st-st, increasing 1 st at neck edge on each side in 1st and every subsequent alternate row until **7**: 8: **8**: 8: **9** increases have been completed in all.
    Break off yarn from right front and slip right front sts back onto right-hand needle point.

Sleeve top shaping

Next row (**Size A only**: inc 1 st at beginning and end of this row): K across left front, *PM, knit up **23**: 24: **26**: 27: **28** sts evenly along edge of work,

PM*, K across back, rep from * to *, K across right front.

Invisibly cast on **32**: 32: **34**: 34: **34** sts. Join work together and work in rounds.

1st round: *K to marker, SM, inc 1, K **23**: 24: **26**: 27: **28**, inc 1, SM*, rep from * to *, K to end.

2nd round: *K to marker, SM, inc 1, K **25**: 26: **28**: 29: **30**, inc 1, SM*, rep from * to *, K to end.

3rd round: *K to marker, SM, inc 1, K **27**: 28: **30**: 31: **32**, inc 1, SM*, rep from * to *, K to end.

4th round: *K to marker, SM, inc 1, K **29**: 30: **32**: 33: **34**, inc 1, SM*, rep from * to *, K to end.

5th round: *K to marker, SM, inc 1, K **31**: 32: **34**: 35: **36**, inc 1, SM*, rep from * to *, K to end.

6th round: *K to marker, SM, inc 1, K **33**: 34: **36**: 37: **38**, inc 1, SM*, rep from * to *, K to end.

7th round: K.

8th round: *K to marker, SM, inc 1, K **35**: 36: **38**: 39: **40**, inc 1, SM*, rep from * to *, K to end.

Continue increasing at armhole markers in alternate rounds until there are **69**: 66: **72**: 67: **70** sts in the sleeve caps (between markers).

To shape the body sections at underarms, increase in next round as follows: *K to 1 st before marker, inc 1, K 1, SM, inc 1, K to next marker, inc 1, SM, K 1, inc 1*, rep from * to *, K to end.

Continue in this manner, increasing at armhole edges as before. At the same, increase as in previous row on fronts and back every alternate row **6**: 8: **9**: 10: **11** more times (**386**: 396: **428**: 426: **440** sts).

This brings the garment to the level of the underarm.

Sleeves

When the sleeve cap and body increases are completed, K 1 round then knit across front to first marker.

***Change to double-pointed needles and knit sleeve sts to 2nd marker, dividing sts on to 3 needles. Invisibly cast on **15**: 16: **18**: 21: **22** sts, placing half the cast-on sts on the first double-pointed needle and half on the third (**98**: 100: **110**: 110: **116** sts).

Thread remaining sts on the circular needle onto a length of left-over yarn, taking care to keep the markers in place.

Continue working the sleeve in rounds until sleeve measures 8 cm, or length desired minus 4 cm.

Work lace edging as follows:

Cast on 10 sts.

***1st row:* K 1, *K 2 tog, yfwd twice*, rep from * to *, K 2 tog, yfwd, K 2, K 2 tog, turn.

2nd row: K 1, K 2 tog, yfwd, K 3, (P 1, K 2) twice.

3rd row: K 1, *K 2 tog, yfwd twice*, rep from * to *, K 2, K 2 tog, yfwd, K 2, K 3 tog, turn.

4th row: K 1, K 2 tog, yfwd, K 5, (P 1, K 2) twice.

5th row: K 1, *K 2 tog, yfwd twice*, rep from * to *, K 4, K 2 tog, yfwd, K 2, K 2 tog, turn.

6th row: K 1, K 2 tog, yfwd, K 7, (P 1, K 2) twice.

7th row: K 11, K 2 tog, yfwd, K 2, K 3 tog, turn.

8th row: K 1, K 2 tog, yfwd, K 13.

Cast off 6 sts. (*Note:* The st left on the right-hand needle point after the casting off will be the first st (K 1) of the first row).**

Rep from ** to ** until all the sleeve sts have been knitted up. Cast off edging.***

Using the circular needle, join in yarn at left-front end of underarm casting on. Knit across cast-on sts. Knit the sts from the length of yarn across the back to the next marker. Rep from *** to ***.

Body

Using the circular needle, Join in yarn at right back end of underarm casting on. Knit across half the cast-on sts, PM, knit the rest of the cast-on sts, then knit up the rest of the sts from the length of yarn (**250**: 260: **280**: 290: **300** sts). Continue working in rounds, keeping the marker in place, until the body is desired length minus 12 cm.

Lace border

1st round: *(yfwd, sl 1, K 1, psso) twice, K 1, (K 2 tog, yfwd) twice, K 1*, rep from * to * to end.

2nd round: K.

3rd round: *K 1, yfwd, sl 1, K 1, psso, yfwd, sl 1, K 2 tog, psso, yfwd, K 2 tog, yfwd, K 2*, rep from * to * to end.

4th round: K.

Rep these 4 rows 7 times. Using one double-pointed needle together with the left-hand end of the circular needle, cast on 10 sts and work lace edging as given for sleeve.

Neckband

Using double-pointed needles, with right side of back facing, and starting at right-hand end of invisible casting on, K **48**: 48: **50**: 50: **52** across back, knit up **16**: 16: **16**: 16: **17** sts evenly down left front edge, K **32**: 32: **34**: 34: **34** sts from front invisible casting on, knit up **16**: 16: **16**: 16: **17** sts evenly up right front edge (**112**: 112: **116**: 116: **120** sts). Divide sts onto 3 needles.

Work 6 rounds in st-st.

Next round: *yfwd, K 2 tog*, rep to end of round.

Work 6 more rounds in st-st and cast off loosely.

Making up

Darn in loose ends. Slip-stitch neckband casting off to beginning of neckband. Stitch cast-on and cast-off ends of lace edgings together. Press lightly.

Lightweight Cardigan

Illustrated on page 85

This set-sleeve cardigan is suitable for cooler days in summer. It features stocking-stitch panels with crosses of crossed stitches on a background of reverse stocking stitch.

Fits chest size (cm)

A	B	C	D	E	F	G
85	90	**95**	100	**105**	110	**115**

Measures (cm)

95	100	**105**	110	**115**	120	**125**

Sleeve length, underarm to wrist (cm)

44	45	**47**	48	**49**	50	**51**

Materials

50 gm balls of 4-ply yarn
8: 8: **8**: 9: **9**: 10: **10** balls
80 cm circular needles and set of four double-pointed needles in sizes 3.25 and 2.75 mm
Cable needle
8 buttons
Small quantity of left-over yarn

Tension

28 sts and 36 rows to 10 cm.

Special abbreviations

C2F: Knit into back of 2nd st on needle, then knit 1st st and slip them off together.
C2B: Knit into front of 2nd st on needle, then knit 1st st and slip them off together.

C3F: Slip next st onto cable needle and hold at front of work. Knit next 2 sts then knit st from cable needle.

INSTRUCTIONS

Begin the work at the back shoulder. Using 3.25 mm circular needle, invisibly cast on **98**: 102: **104**: 106: **110**: 112: **116** sts.

1st row: K **4**: 5: **6**: 6: **6**: 6: **7**, P 9, K 8, P 9, K **38**: 40: **40**: 42: **46**: 48: **50**, P 9, K 8, P 9, K **4**: 5: **6**: 6: **6**: 6: **7**.

2nd row: P **4**: 5: **6**: 6: **6**: 6: **7**, K 9, P 8, K 9, P **38**: 40: **40**: 42: **46**: 48: **50**, K **8**: 7: **8**: 8: **6**: 6: **7**, turn (see page 11).

3rd row: P **8**: 7: **8**: 8: **6**: 6: **7**, K **38**: 40: **40**: 42: **46**: 48: **50**, P **8**: 7: **8**: 8: **6**: 6: **7**, turn.

4th row: K **8**: 7: **8**: 8: **6**: 6: **7**, P **38**: 40: **40**: 42: **46**: 48: **50**, K 9, P 8, K **2**: 2: **3**: 3: **2**: 2: **3**, turn.

5th row: P **2**: 2: **3**: 3: **2**: 2: **3**, K 8, P 9, K **38**: 40: **40**: 42: **46**: 48: **50**, P 9, K 8, P **2**: 2: **3**: 3: **2**: 2: **3**, turn.

6th row: K **2**: 2: **3**: 3: **2**: 2: **3**, P 8, K 9, P **38**: 40: **40**: 42: **46**: 48: **50**, K 9, P 8, K 9, P **4**: 5: **6**: 6: **6**: 6: **7**.

7th row: K **4**: 5: **6**: 6: **6**: 6: **7**, P 9, K 8, P 9, K **38**: 40: **40**: 42: **46**: 48: **50**, P 9, K 8, P 9, K **4**: 5: **6**: 6: **6**: 6: **7**.

8th row: P **4**: 5: **6**: 6: **6**: 6: **7**, *C2F, K 5, C2B, P 8, C2F, K 5, C2B*, P **38**: 40: **40**: 42: **46**: 48: **50**, rep from * to *, P **4**: 5: **6**: 6: **6**: 6: **7**.

9th and alternate rows: K **4**: 5: **6**: 6: **6**: 6: **7**, P 9, K 8, P 9, K **38**: 40: **40**: 42: **46**: 48: **50**, P 9, K 8, P 9, K **4**: 5: **6**: 6: **6**: 6: **7**.

10th row: P **4**: 5: **6**: 6: **6**: 6: **7**, *K 1, C2F, K 3, C2B, K 1, P 8, K 1, C2F, K 3, C2B, K 1*, P **38**: 40: **40**: 42: **46**: 48: **50**, rep from * to *, P **4**: 5: **6**: 6: **6**: 6: **7**.

12th row: P **4**: 5: **6**: 6: **6**: 6: **7**, *K 2, C2F, K 1, C2B, K 2, P 8, K 2, C2F, K 1, C2B, K 2*, P **38**: 40: **40**: 42: **46**: 48: **50**, rep from * to *, P **4**: 5: **6**: 6: **6**: 6: **7**.

14th row: P **4**: 5: **6**: 6: **6**: 6: **7**, *K 3, C3F, K 3, P 8, K 3, C3F, K 3*, P **38**: 40: **40**: 42: **46**: 48: **50**, rep from * to *, P **4**: 5: **6**: 6: **6**: 6: **7**.

16th row: P **4**: 5: **6**: 6: **6**: 6: **7**, *K 2, C2B, K 1, C2F, K 2, P 8, K 2, C2B, K 1, C2F, K 2*, P **38**: 40: **40**: 42: **46**: 48: **50**, rep from * to *, P **4**: 5: **6**: 6: **6**: 6: **7**.

18th row: P **4**: 5: **6**: 6: **6**: 6: **7**, *K 1, C2B, K 3, C2F, K 1, P 8, K 1, C2B, K 3, C2F, K 1*, P **38**: 40: **40**: 42: **46**: 48: **50**, rep from * to *, P **4**: 5: **6**: 6: **6**: 6: **7**.

20th row: P **4**: 5: **6**: 6: **6**: 6: **7**, *C2B, K 5, C2F, P 8, C2B, K 5, C2F*, P **38**: 40: **40**: 42: **46**: 48: **50**, rep from * to *, P **4**: 5: **6**: 6: **6**: 6: **7**.

21st row: As 9th row.

22nd row: P **4**: 5: **6**: 6: **6**: 6: **7**, K 9, P 8, K 9, P **38**: 40: **40**: 42: **46**: 48: **50**, K 9, P 8, K 9, P **4**: 5: **6**: 6: **6**: 6: **7**.

23rd row: As 9th row.

Rep 22nd and 23rd rows **0**: 1: **1**: 1: **2**: 1: **2** more times. Break off yarn, leave sts on circular needle.

Front shoulders

With right side of work facing and using the right-hand end of circular needle, pick up and knit **34**: 36: **37**: 37: **38**: 38: **40** sts from invisible casting on (right front). Using a second ball of yarn, miss **30**: 30: **30**: 32: **34**: 36: **36** sts, join in yarn and knit up **34**: 36: **37**: 37: **38**: 38: **40** sts (left front).

1st row: Left front: K **4**: 5: **6**: 6: **6**: 6: **7**, P 9, K 8, P 9, K **4**: 5: **5**: 5: **6**: 6: **7**. Right front: K **4**: 5: **5**: 5: **6**: 6: **7**, P 9, K 8, P 9, K **4**: 5: **6**: 6: **6**: 6: **7**.

2nd row: Right front: P **4**: 5: **6**: 6: **6**: 6: **7**, K 9, P 8, K 9, P **4**: 5: **5**: 5: **6**: 6: **7**. Left front: P **4**: 5: **5**: 5: **6**: 6: **7**, K 8: 7: **8**: 8: **6**: 6: **7**, turn.

3rd row: Left front: P **8**: 7: **8**: 8: **6**: 6: **7**, K **4**: 5: **5**: 5: **6**: 6: **7**. Right front: K **4**: 5: **5**: 5: **6**: 6: **7**, P **8**: 7: **8**: 8: **6**: 6: **7**, turn.

4th row: Right front: K **8**: 7: **8**: 8: **6**: 6: **7**, P **4**: 5: **5**: 5: **6**: 6: **7**. Left front: P **4**: 5: **5**: 5: **6**: 6: **7**, K 9, P 8, K **1**: 2: **2**: 2: **3**: 3: **2**, turn.

5th row: Left front: P **1**: 2: **2**: 2: **3**: 3: **2**, K 8, P 9, K **4**: 5: **5**: 5: **6**: 6: **7**. Right front: K **4**: 5: **5**: 5: **6**: 6: **7**, P 9, K 8, P **1**: 2: **2**: 2: **3**: 3: **2**, turn.

6th row: Right front: K **1**: 2: **2**: 2: **3**: 3: **2**, P 8, K 9, P **4**: 5: **5**: 5: **6**: 6: **7**. Left front: P **4**: 5: **5**: 5: **6**: 6: **7**, K 9, P 8, K 9, P **4**: 5: **6**: 6: **6**: 6: **7**.

7th row: Left front: K **4**: 5: **6**: 6: **6**: 6: **7**, P 9, K 8, P 9, K **4**: 5: **5**: 5: **6**: 6: **7**. Right front: K **4**: 5: **5**: 5: **6**: 6: **7**, P 9, K 8, P 9, K **4**: 5: **6**: 6: **6**: 6: **7**.

Working across both right and left fronts, work **16**: 18: **18**: 18: **20**: 18: **20** more rows in pattern, beginning crossed stitch pattern in next row as for back (rows 8 to 21).

Break off yarn from right front and slip the right-front sts onto the right-hand end of the circular needle.

Sleeve top and neck shaping

Work the sleeve top shaping as given in the following 8 rows while continuing the pattern on the fronts and back. Work the next set of crossed-stitch pattern rows (as in rows 8 to 21 of the back) after completing 14 rows from the end of the last crossed-stitch pattern, then repeat the 14 rows as in rows 8 to 21 of the back.

1st row: P 1, inc 1 P, work across left front, *PM, knit up **25**: 27: **27**: 28: **29**: 28: **29** sts evenly along edge of work, PM*, work across back, rep from * to *, work across right front to last st, inc 1 P, P 1.

2nd row: *Work to marker, SM, inc 1, K **25**: 27: **27**: 28: **29**: 28: **29**, inc 1, SM*, rep from * to *, work to end.

3rd row: P 1, inc 1 P, *work to marker, SM, inc 1 P, P **27**: 29: **29**: 30: **31**: 30: **31**, inc 1 P, SM*, rep from * to *, work to last st, inc 1 P, P 1.

4th row: *Work to marker, SM, inc 1, K **29**: 31: **31**: 32: **33**: 32: **33**, inc 1, SM*, rep from * to *, work to end.

5th row: P 1, inc 1 P, *work to marker, SM, inc 1 P, P **31**: 33: **33**: 34: **34**: 34: **35**, inc 1 P, SM*, rep from * to *, work to last st, inc 1 P, P 1.

6th row: *Work to marker, SM, inc 1, K **33**: 35: **35**: 36: **37**: 36: **37**, inc 1, SM*, rep from * to *, work to end.

7th row: P 1, inc 1 P, *work to marker, SM, inc 1 P, P **35**: 37: **37**: 38: **39**: 38: **39**, inc 1 P, SM*, rep from * to *, work to last st, inc 1 P, P 1.

8th row: Work without shaping.

Continue in this manner, increasing at armhole markers next and every alternate row and at neck edge until **7**: 7: **7**: 8: **8**: 9: **9** neck edge increases have been completed. Work 1 row. At end of next 2 rows, invisibly cast on **8**: 8: **8**: 8: **9**: 9: **9** sts.

Continue working in rows, increasing at sleeve markers in alternate rows until there are **69**: 71: **69**: 72: **73**: 74: **75** sts in sleeve caps (between markers).

To shape the body sections at underarms, increase in next row as follows: *Work to 1 st before marker, inc 1 P, K 1, SM, inc 1 P, work to next marker, inc 1 P, SM, K 1, inc 1 P*, rep from * to *, work to end.

Continue in this manner, increasing at armhole edges as before. At the same time, increase as in previous row on fronts and back every alternate row **8**: 9: **10**: 11: **12**: 13: **14** more times (**406**: 424: **434**: 456: **470**: 484: **502** sts).

Work 1 row (wrong side), then work across left front to 1st marker.

Left sleeve

Change to 3.25 mm double-pointed needles and work sleeve sts to 2nd marker, dividing sts evenly onto 3 needles. Invisibly cast on **17: 19: **21**: 22: **25**: 28: **29** sts, placing half on the first double-pointed needle and half on the third (**104**: 110: **112**: 118: **124**: 130: **134** sts).

Thread remaining sts on the circular needle onto

Lightweight woman's cardigan (page 83)

Colourful T-shaped sweater for a baby (page 100)

Woman's cardigan with square-set sleeve (page 93)

Chequerboard jacket (page 98)

Sideways-knitted vest (page 104)
worn with a very simple ribbed
skirt (page 109)

a length of left-over yarn, taking care to keep the markers in place.

Continue working the sleeve in rounds until sleeve measures 5 cm.

Next round: P 1, P 2 tog, P to last 3 sts, P 2 tog, P 1.

Decrease in this manner every 6th round until **62**: 68: **66**: 72: **76**: 82: **84** sts remain. Work 5 rounds without shaping.

Next round: Decrease **2**: 8: **4**: 8: **8**: 14: **14** sts evenly over round (**60**: 60: **62**: 64: **68**: 68: **70** sts).

Change to 2.75 mm double-pointed needles and work in K 1, P 1 rib for 5 cm. Cast off loosely in rib.**

Right sleeve

Using the circular needle, join in yarn at left-front end of underarm casting on. Work across cast-on sts. Work the sts from the length of yarn across the back to next marker. Rep from ** to **.

Body

Using the 3.25 mm circular needle, join in yarn at right-back end of underarm casting on. Work across cast-on sts, then work the rest of the sts from the length of yarn (**266**: 282: **294**: 308: **322**: 336: **350** sts).

Continue working in pattern until the body is desired length minus 5 cm, ending with a wrong-side row (if possible the last row of the crossed-stitch pattern).

Change to 2.75 mm circular needle and work in K 1, P 1 rib for 5 cm. Cast off loosely in rib.

Neckband

Using 2.75 mm circular needle, with right side of work facing and starting at right front invisible casting on, knit up **8**: 8: **8**: 8: **9**: 9: **9** sts from casting on, then pick up **28**: 28: **28**: 30: **30**: 31: **31** sts evenly up right side. Knit up **30**: 30: **30**: 32: **34**: 36: **36** sts from back neck casting on, then **28**: 28: **28**: 30: **30**: 31: **31** sts down left side and **8**: 8: **8**: 8: **9**: 9: **9** sts from left front casting on (**102**: 102: **102**: 108: **112**: 116: **116** sts).

Work 10 rows in K 1, P 1 rib. Cast off loosely in rib.

Front bands

Using 2.75 mm circular needle, with right side of work facing and starting at lower edge of right front, pick up 1 st for each row to top edge of neckband. Work 5 rows in K 1, P 1 rib.

Next row: Rib 4, cast off 3 sts for buttonhole. Work 7 more buttonholes evenly spaced between bottom edge and neckband (see page 14).

Next row: Rib to 1st buttonhole. Cast on 3 sts over each buttonhole.

Work 5 more rows in rib. Cast off loosely in rib.

Work left front band to correspond, omitting buttonholes.

Making up

Darn in loose ends. Sew on buttons. Press if desired.

Set-sleeve Sweater or Cardigan

First make a tension sample (see page 10) and take measurements (see page 11).

Convert the following measurements into numbers of sts, calculated from your tension sample: chest, upper arm, wrist, shoulders.

Next calculate the number of back-neck sts. If you wish to have a V-neck sweater or a low-buttoning cardigan, follow the instructions for this calculation in the Design Instructions for the Saddle-shoulder Sweater on page 43. If you wish to have a round neck or a high-buttoning cardigan, the back neck should be one-third the shoulder measurement (you can make it wider if you wish).

To calculate the underarm cast-ons, subtract twice the number of shoulder sts from the number of chest sts and divide the result by 4.

The sleeve cap can now be divided into four separate components: the sleeve top, 5 rows with increases every row, a number of rows with increases every alternate row, and the underarm cast-ons.

First determine the number of rows in the alternate-row increases in the sleeve cap shaping. From the total number of sts in the upper arm measurement subtract the number of sts in the sleeve top (one-third of the upper-arm sts minus 10), the underarm cast-ons, and 10 (the number of sts added in the even-row increases)†. This will give the number of sts to be added in the alternate-row increases; as there are 2 sts added every second row, it will also give the number of rows in the alternate-row increases.

To obtain the total number of rows in the sleeve cap shapings, add 5 to the number of rows in the alternate-row increases.

---

†The reason behind subtracting 10 from the sleeve-top sts and adding 10 sts in every-row increases is to give the sleeve top a more smoothly rounded shape.

Back

Next calculate the number of sts required for the shoulder side (shoulder sts minus back neck sts divided by 2).

Using a circular needle, invisibly cast on the calculated number of sts for the shoulders. Purl 1 row.

Now shape the shoulders. Work across the right shoulder and back neck sts then work one-third of the left shoulder sts and turn (see page 11). Purl back across the left shoulder and neck sts, purl one-third of the right shoulder sts and turn. Knit back to left shoulder, knit two-thirds of the sts and turn. Continue in this manner until all the sts have been knitted up.

Next a number of rows have to be worked without shaping. To calculate this number, divide the calculated number of sleeve-top sts by 2 and multiply the result by 3 (thus converting sts to rows), then divide this number by 2.

Work the calculated number of rows then break off yarn and leave sts on the circular needle.

Front

Join in yarn at right-hand end of invisible casting on and pick up the calculated number of sts for the shoulder side. Miss the back neck sts, then pick up left shoulder side sts.

Purl 1 row on both sides, then shape the shoulders in the manner given for the back. Finish with a purl row across both fronts. Break off yarn from right front and slip right-front sts onto the right-hand end of the circular needle.

Sleeve top and neck shaping

Work across left front, *PM, pick up the calculated number of sleeve-top sts along side edge of front and back, PM*, work across back, rep from * to *, work across right front.

Work 5 rows, increasing on the armhole sides of the markers in every row, then increase every alternate row.

At the same time, the increases for the neck are worked. If you wish to have a V-neck or a low-buttoning cardigan, refer to the Design Instructions for the Saddle-shoulder Sweater on page 43. If you want a round neck or a high-buttoning cardigan, begin the neck increases about 5 cm from the shoulder, or less if you want a shallow neckline. To calculate the number of increases, divide the back neck sts by 4. When these increases are completed, invisibly cast on half the number of back neck sts, join the work together and work in rounds. If you are making a cardigan, invisibly cast on half this number of sts at the end of the next 2 rows and continue the work in rows.

It will now be necessary to make another calculation. The previously calculated number of sts will have to be added at the underarm, and the body will have to be shaped at the bottom of the armhole. The number of sts to be added in the body shaping on each side of each armhole will be half the number of underarm cast ons.

From the calculated number of upper arm sts, subtract the underarm cast ons and twice the number of body increases. Continue the alternate row increases on the armhole until you have this number of sts in the sleeve cap. Continue the sleeve-cap increases as before, at the same time increasing also on the body sides of the markers for the number of times you have calculated for the body increases, the last body increase coinciding with the last armhole increase.

Sleeves

Work 1 more round, then break off yarn and slip left-front sts (to marker) onto right-hand needle point. Using a set of double-pointed needles, work across sleeve sts then invisibly cast on the number of sts which you have calculated for the underarm cast-ons. Place half the cast-on sts on the first double-pointed needle and half on the third.

If you wish to have a short sleeve, work in rounds until the sleeve is desired length and finish it with your choice of edging stitch.

If you wish to have a long sleeve, work as follows:

Work in rounds for 5 cm, then decrease at each end of every 4th or 6th round until the sleeve is the required length minus 5 cm.

To work out the correct decreasing intervals to make the sleeve the correct length, first calculate the number of rows in the shaped part of the sleeve (sleeve length minus 10 cm). Subtract the wrist sts from the upper arm sts and divide the result by 2.

This will give you the number of decreasing rows. Divide the calculated number of rows in the shaped part of the sleeve first by 4 and then by 6. Choose whichever result is closest to the number of wrist sts but not less than that number. On the last round, decrease any excess sts evenly over the round so that the final number is equal to the number of sts required for the wrist.

Change to smaller sized double-pointed needles and work 5 cm in rib.

Join in yarn at left-front end of underarm casting on, work across cast-on sts then work across back to next marker. Work another sleeve to correspond.

Body

Join in yarn at right-back end of underarm casting on. Work across the cast-on sts then work the front sts. Continue working in rounds for a sweater or rows for a cardigan until the body is desired length minus whatever width you wish your basque to be. Finish with your choice of stitch, using a smaller circular needle if you are finishing with ribbing.

If you are making a cardigan and you wish it to have pockets, refer to the Design Instructions for the Cardigan with Square-set Sleeve on page 97.

Neckband

If you are using ribbing for the neckband, use smaller sized double-pointed needles. Knit up neck sts from invisible casting on, then pick up 3 sts for every 4 rows down left side. If you are making a round-neck sweater or a high-buttoning cardigan, knit up sts from invisible casting on, then pick up the same number of sts on the right side. If you are making a V-neck sweater, follow the instructions given in the Design Instructions for the Saddle-shoulder Sweater on page 43.

Work the neckband to the desired width in your chosen stitch, then cast off loosely.

Cardigan front bands

Low-buttoning cardigan: Using smaller sized circular needle, with right side of work facing and starting at lower edge of right front, pick up 1 st for each row up right side to last neck increase, then 3 sts for every 4 rows along shaped edge. Knit up sts from invisible casting on at back neck. Pick up 3 sts for every 4 rows along shaped edge of left front, then 1 st for each row to bottom edge. Work in rib for desired width, working buttonholes at regular intervals between bottom edge and beginning of neck shaping in the centre of the band (on the right side for a woman's cardigan and on the left side for a man's). Cast off loosely in rib.

High-buttoning cardigan: Using smaller sized circular needle, with right side of work facing and starting at lower edge of right front, pick up 1 st for each row up right side to top of neckband. Work in rib, working buttonholes at regular intervals between bottom edge and beginning of neck shaping in centre of band. Cast off loosely in rib.

Work left-front band to correspond, omitting buttonholes.

Making up

Darn in loose ends. Sew buttons on cardigan. Press if desired.

Woman's Cardigan with Square-set Sleeve

Illustrated on page 86

This comfortable cardigan in 8-ply yarn features rib-and-cable basque, cuffs and pocket-tops, with a similar trim at the top of the sleeves.

Fits chest size (cm)

A	B	C	D	E	F	G	H
85	90	**95**	100	**105**	110	**115**	120

Measures (cm)

95	100	**105**	110	**115**	120	**125**	130

Sleeve length, underarm to wrist (cm)

44	45	**47**	48	**49**	50	**51**	52

Materials

50 gm balls of 8-ply yarn
13: 13: **14**: 15: **16**: 17: **18**: 18 balls
80 cm circular needles and sets of four double-pointed needles in sizes 4 mm and 3.25 mm
6 buttons
Small quantity of left-over yarn

Tension

22 sts and 30 rows to 10 cm, measured over stocking stitch, using 4 mm needles.

Special abbreviation

C2F: K into back of 2nd st on needle, K 1st st then slip both sts off together.

INSTRUCTIONS

Begin the work at the back shoulders. Using 4 mm circular needle, invisibly cast on **88**: 94: **100**: 106: **110**: 116: **122**: 128 sts.
1st row: P.
2nd row: K **68**: 74: **78**: 82: **86**: 90: **96**: 100, turn (see page 11).
3rd row: P **48**: 54: **56**: 58: **62**: 64: **70**: 72, turn.
4th row: K **58**: 64: **67**: 70: **74**: 77: **83**: 86, turn.
5th row: P **68**: 74: **78**: 82: **86**: 90: **96**: 100, turn.
6th row: K to end.
7th row: P.
 Work **74**: 75: **78**: 78: **81**: 81: **87**: 87 more rows in st-st. Break off yarn, thread sts onto a length of left-over yarn.

Front shoulders

With right side of work facing and using the circular needle, pick up and knit **29**: 31: **33**: 35: **36**: 38: **40**: 42 sts from invisible casting on (right front). Using a second ball of yarn, miss **30**: 32: **34**: 36: **38**: 40: **42**: 44 sts, join in yarn and knit up **29**: 31: **33**: 35: **36**: 38: **40**: 42 sts (left front).
1st row: P across left and right fronts.
2nd row: K back across right front, K **9**: 11: **11**: 11: **12**: 12: **14**: 14 on left front, turn.
3rd row: P back across left front, P **9**: 11: **11**: 11: **12**: 12: **14**: 14 on right front, turn.
4th row: K back across right front, K **20**: 20: **22**: 24: **24**: 26: **26**: 28 on left front, turn.
5th row: P back across left front, P **20**: 20: **22**: 24: **24**: 26: **26**: 28 on right front, turn.
6th row: K back across right front, K to end of left front.
7th row: P across left front, P to end of right front.
 Working across both right and left front, work

16: 12: **10**: 6: **6**: 2: **4**: 0 more rows in st-st.
Next row: Inc 1 st at centre front edges of right and left front.

Continue working in st-st, increasing at front edges in 3rd and every following 4th rows until there are **44**: 47: **50**: 53: **55**: 58: **61**: 64 sts on each side.

Work 3 rows without shaping. Thread sts onto a length of left-over yarn.

Sleeves

Using 4 mm circular needle, with right side of work facing, beginning at lower edge of left front, pick up **102**: 104: **108**: 108: **112**: 112: **120**: 120 sts evenly along left armhole edge. (Pick up approximately 2 sts for every 3 rows.)
1st row: (K 2, P 2) to end.
2nd row: **Sizes A, C and D**: *K 2, P 2, C2F, P 2*, rep from * to * to last 4 sts, K 2, P 2. **Sizes B, E, F, G and H**: *K 2, P 2, C2F, P 2*, rep from * to * to end.
3rd and 4th rows: As 1st and 2nd rows.
Repeat these 4 rows twice.
Change to 4 mm double-pointed needles. Divide sts evenly onto 3 needles and work in rounds in st-st until sleeve measures 5 cm.
Next round: K 1, K 2 tog, work to last 3 sts, sl 1, K 1, psso, K 1.
Decrease in this manner every **4th**: 4th: **4th**: 4th: **6th**: 6th: **6th**: 6th round until 48: 50: 52: 52: 72: 72: 78: 78 sts remain.
Work **3**: 3: **3**: 3: **5**: 5: **5**: 5 rounds without shaping.
Next round: Decrease **4**: 2: **4**: 0: **16**: 16: **18**: 18 sts evenly over round (**44**: 48: **48**: 52: **56**: 56: **60**: 60 sts).
Change to 3.25 mm double-pointed needles and work cuff as follows:
1st and 2nd rounds: (K 2, P 2) to end.
3rd round: **Sizes A, D, G and H**: *K 2, P 2, C2F, P 2*, rep from * to * last 4 sts, K 2, P 2. **Sizes B, C, E and F**: *K 2, P 2, C2F, P 2*, rep from * to * end.
4th round: As 1st and 2nd rounds.
Repeat these 4 rounds 3 times. Cast off loosely in rib.
Work right sleeve to correspond.

Body

Replace front and back sts on the 4 mm circular needle. Rejoin yarn at left centre front and knit across left front. Pick up **16**: 16: **16**: 14: **16**: 16: **16**: 15 sts along unjoined edges of left sleeve, knit across back, pick up **16**: 16: **16**: 14: **16**: 16: **16**: 15 sts along unjoined edges of right sleeve, then knit across right front (**208**: 220: **232**: 240: **252**: 264: **276**: 286 sts).
Next row: P.

Continue working in st-st until body is desired length minus 15 cm, ending with a wrong-side row.
Next row: K **15**: 17: **18**: 19: **21**: 22: **24**: 25. *Using a piece of contrasting yarn, K 22, then slip these sts back onto the left-hand needle point. Knit across these contrasting sts*. K **134**: 142: **152**: 158: **166**: 176: **184**: 192, rep from * to *, K to end.

Work 10 cm more in st-st, ending with a wrong-side row.

Change to 3.25 mm circular needle and work as follows:
1st and 2nd rows: (K 2, P 2) to end.
3rd row: **Sizes B, E and G**: *K 2, P 2, C2F, P 2*, rep from * to * to last 4 sts, K 2, P 2. **Size H**: *K 2, P 2, C2F, P 2*, rep from * to * to last 6 sts, K 2, P 2, K 2. **Sizes A, C, D and F**: *K 2, P 2, C2F, P 2*, rep from * to * to end.
4th row: As 1st and 2nd rows.
Repeat these 4 rows 3 times.
Cast off loosely in rib.

Pockets

Carefully pull out contrasting yarn. Using 4 mm double-pointed needles, with right sides facing, pick up 22 sts from bottom of slit, 1 st at side, 22 sts at top of slit, and 1 st at side. (*Note:* This procedure is safer and easier if a smaller sized needle is threaded through the sts to be picked up before the contrasting yarn is pulled out.) Divide the sts on to 3 needles and work 10 cm in st-st. Divide again on to 2 needles (top sts on one needle, bottom sts on the other) and carefully turn pockets inside out. With needles side by side, right sides of work together, using a third needle, knit the first sts on the back and front needles together, then knit the second sts and cast off the first. Continue in this manner until all the sts are cast off. Fold pocket down.

Using 3.25 mm needles, pick up 22 sts along top of fold, taking care to keep an even line. Work as follows, at the end of each row picking up 1 st from the body close to the pocket top and knitting it together with the last st.
1st row: (K 2, P 2) to last 2 sts, K 2.
2nd row: *P 2, C2F, P 2, K 2*, rep from * to *, P 2, C2F, P 2.
3rd row: As 2nd row.
4th row: (P 2, K 2) to last 2 sts, P 2.
Rep 1st to 3rd rows then cast off loosely in rib.

Band

Using 3.25 mm circular needle, with right side of work facing and starting at lower edge of right front, pick up 1 st for each row up right side to last neck increase, then 3 sts for every 4 rows along shaped edge. Knit up **30**: 32: **34**: 36: **38**: 40: **42**: 44 sts from invisible casting on along back neck. Pick up 3 sts for every 4 rows along shaped edge of left front, then 1 st for each row to bottom edge.

Work 5 rows in K 2, P 2 rib.

Next row: Rib 4, cast off 3 sts for buttonhole. Work 5 more buttonholes evenly spaced between bottom edge and beginning of neck shaping (see page 14).

Next row: Rib to 1st buttonhole. Cast on 3 sts over each buttonhole.

Work 4 more rows in rib. Cast off loosely in rib.

Making up

Darn in loose ends. Sew on buttons. Press if desired.

Cardigan with Square-set Sleeve

First make a tension sample (see page 10) and take measurements (see page 11).

Back

Begin at the back shoulders. Calculate the number of sts to cast on from your shoulder measurement. This measurement may be slightly wider than the measurement for a set-sleeve garment. Invisibly cast on this number of sts and use markers to divide them into three sections: right shoulder, back neck and left shoulder. The back neck should be about one-third of the shoulder measurement.

The next step is to shape the shoulders. Work across the left shoulder and neck, then work one-third of the right shoulder sts and turn (see page 11). Work back across these sts and the neck sts, then work one-third of the left shoulder sts and turn. Work back to right shoulder and work two-thirds of the sts and turn. Continue in this manner until all the sts have been knitted up.

Work until the back measures half your upper arm measurement.

Front shoulders

With right side of work facing and using the circular needle, pick up and knit the shoulder sts on the right front from the invisible casting on. Using a second ball of yarn, miss the neck sts, join in yarn and pick up the left shoulder sts from the invisible casting on.

Work shoulder shapings to correspond with the back.

Work a few rows without shaping, then commence the neck shaping. Increase 1 st at neck edge in every 4th row until the number of sts on each front equals half the number of back sts (in other words, the number of sts added to each front equals half the back neck sts).

When the fronts are the same length as the back, break off yarn and thread sts on to a length of left-over yarn.

Sleeves

First calculate from your stitch tension the number of sts required for the upper arm measurement. This gives the number of sts to be picked up along the side of the fronts and back.

Using double-pointed needles, with right side of work facing and starting at bottom edge of left front, pick up the previously calculated number of sts along the side of the front. If the measurements and calculations are correct, this should come to approximately 2 sts for every 3 rows. Pick up the same number of sts along the side of the back.

Before going any further, calculate the number of sts required for the chest measurement. Subtract the total number of sts now on the back and the fronts and divide the result by 2. This will give the number of sts to be added to complete the body.

Convert this figure from sts into rows by dividing it by 2 and multiplying the result by 3, then divide this again by 2. (*Example:* Sts required to complete the body = 20; divide by 2 = 10; multiply by 3 = 30; divide by 2 = 15.)

Work this calculated number of rows without shaping, using a different stitch pattern if desired, then join the sleeve st together and work in rounds.

Work about 5 cm without shaping, then decrease at each end of every 4th or 6th round until the sleeve is 5 cm less than the desired length.

To work out the correct decreasing intervals to make the sleeve the correct length, first calculate the number of rows in the shaped part of the sleeve (sleeve length minus 10 cm). Subtract the wrist sts from the upper arm sts and divide the result by 2. This will give you the number of decreasing rows. Divide the calculated number of rows in the shaped part of the sleeve first by 4 and then by 6. Choose whichever result is closest to the number of wrist sts but not less than that number. Subtract that number from the number of sts still on the needles. On the last round before working the cuff, decrease the excess number evenly over the round.

Change to smaller sized needles and work 5 cm in rib. Cast off loosely in rib.

Body

Replace the front and back sts on the circular needle. Rejoin yarn at left centre front and work across left front. Pick up along unjoined edges of left sleeve half the calculated number of sts required to complete the body. This should work out at 2 sts for every 3 rows. Work across back then pick up the same number of sts along unjoined edge of right sleeve and work across right front.

Continue working in rows until the body is the desired length minus 15 cm, ending with a wrong-side row.

The next step is to knit in a piece of contrasting yarn for later placing of the pockets. The pocket should be approximately 10 cm in width. Decide on the position of the pocket, then work up to that point. Using a piece of contrasting yarn, knit across the pocket sts then slip these sts back onto the left-hand needle. Work across these sts in pattern. Work right front to correspond.

Work another 10 cm, ending with a wrong-side row.

Change to smaller sized circular needle and work in rib for 5 cm. Cast off loosely in rib.

Pockets

Carefully pull out contrasting yarn. Using double-pointed needles, with right sides facing, pick up the same number of sts as worked on the contrasting yarn from bottom of slit, 1 st at side, the same number of sts at top of slit, and 1 st at side. (*Note:* This procedure is safer and easier if a smaller sized needle is threaded through the sts to be picked up before the contrasting yarn is pulled out.) Divide the sts onto 3 needles and work 10 cm in st-st. Divide again onto 2 needles (top sts on one needle, bottom sts on the other) and carefully turn pockets inside out. With needles side by side, right sides of work together, using a third needle, knit the first sts on the back and front needles together, then knit the second sts and cast off the first. Continue in this manner until all the sts are cast off. Fold pocket down.

Using smaller-sized needles, pick up the number of pocket sts along top of fold, taking care to keep an even line. Work 8 rows in rib. At the end of each row, pick up 1 st from the body close to the pocket top and knit it together with the last st. Cast off loosely in rib.

Band

Using smaller sized circular needle, with right side of work facing and starting at lower edge of right front, pick up 1 st for each row up right side to last neck increase, then 3 sts for every 4 rows along shaped edge. Knit up sts from invisible casting on of right saddle, back neck and left saddle. Pick up 3 sts for every 4 rows along shaped edge of left front, then 1 st for each row to bottom edge.

Work 10 rows in rib, working buttonholes at regular intervals between bottom edge and beginning of neck shaping in 5th and 6th rows. Cast off loosely in rib.

Making up

Darn in loose ends. Sew on buttons. Press if desired.

Chequerboard Jacket

Illustrated on page 87

This long buttoned jacket is designed for cold weather. A simple T-shape, it is worked in double 8-ply yarn in a chequerboard pattern and features wide garter stitch bands and a deep collar.

Fits chest size (cm)

A	B	C	D
85	90	**95**	100

Measures (cm)

95	100	**105**	110

Sleeve length, underarm to wrist (cm)

43	44	**46**	47

Materials

50 gm balls of 8-ply yarn (used double throughout)
23: 25: **27**: 28 balls
80 cm circular needle in size 6 mm
2 stitch-holders
4 large buttons
Small quantity of left-over yarn

Tension

16 sts and 22 rows to 10 cm, measured over st-st.

INSTRUCTIONS

The work begins at the lower edge. *Double yarn* is used throughout.

Cast on **142**: 158: **166**: 174 sts and work 14 rows in garter st, then begin chequerboard pattern.

1st row: K 7, (K 8, P 8) to last **7**: 7: **15**: 7 sts, K **7**: 7: **15**: 7.

2nd row: K **7**: 7: **15**: 7, (P 8, K 8) to last 7 sts, K 7.

Rep 1st and 2nd row 4 times.

11th row: K 7, (P 8, K 8) to last **7**: 7: **15**: 7 sts, P **7**: 7: **15**: 7, K 7.

12th row: K 7, P **7**: 7: **15**: 7, (K 8, P 8) to last 7 sts, K 7.

Rep 11th and 12th row 4 times.

Continue working in chequerboard pattern with garter st border for 18 cm, ending with a wrong-side row.

Next row: K 2, cast off 3 for buttonhole, K 2, work in pattern to end.

Next row: Work in pattern to last 7 sts, K 2, cast on 3, K 2.

Work 3 more buttonholes at 10 cm intervals, then work 2 cm, ending with a wrong-side row.

Back and sleeves

Keeping continuity of pattern, work **35**: 39: **41**: 43 sts. Thread these sts on to a length of left-over yarn.

Invisibly cast on **61**: 64: **70**: 68 sts. Work back in pattern, working 1st 7 sts in garter st, then work **72**: 80: **84**: 88 in pattern and invisibly cast on **61**: 64: **70**: 68 sts (**194**: 208: **224**: 224 sts). Thread last **35**: 39: **41**: 43 sts on to a length of left-over yarn.

Keeping continuity of pattern and working first and last 7 sts of each row in garter st, work **32**: 32: **34**: 36 rows.

Shape sleeve top and shoulder

1st row: Work to last **19**: 27: **24**: 22 sts, turn.
2nd row: Work to last **19**: 28: **25**: 23 sts, turn.
3rd row: Work to last **26**: 33: **31**: 29 sts, turn.
4th row: Work to last **26**: 34: **32**: 30 sts, turn.

Keeping continuity of pattern, continue in this manner, working **7**: 6: **7**: 7 less sts each row, until **30**: 35: **35**: 39 sts remain. Place these sts on a stitch-holder and thread remaining sts on to a length of left-over yarn.

Front and sleeves

Replace right front sts on circular needle. With right side facing, knit up **61**: 64: **70**: 68 sts from invisible casting on. Work back to left sleeve, knit up **61**: 64: **70**: 68 sts from invisible casting on.

Work sleeve as for back, keeping continuity of pattern and garter st border and working top shaping to correspond.

Join the sleeve and shoulder sts together by one of the methods described in the Joining Shoulders section of Special Techniques on page 12.

Leave remaining front sts on a stitch-holder.

Replace left front sts on circular needle and work left front and sleeve to correspond.

Collar

Replace sts from stitch-holder on circular needle. Keeping continuity of garter st border, work 10 cm in pattern, then work 14 rows in garter st. Cast off.

Making up

Darn in loose ends. Using double yarn, crochet 2 rows of double crochet around lower edge, front edges and collar and around ends of sleeves. Sew on buttons. Do not press.

Baby's T-shaped Sweater

Illustrated on page 85

This simple T-shaped sweater in multi-coloured stripes is designed to fit a one- to two-year-old child.

Chest size

58 cm (actual measurement)

Sleeve length

14 cm

Materials

50 gm balls of 8-ply yarn: 2 balls in main colour (M), 1 ball each in 4 contrasting colours (C1, C2, C3 and C4).
40-cm circular needle and set of four double-pointed needles in size 4 mm.
Small quantity of left-over yarn
3 stitch-holders
1 button

Tension

22 sts and 30 rows to 10 cm.

INSTRUCTIONS

Using the thumb method and M, cast on 128 sts (see page 11). Before going any further check that there is no twist in the casting on. Place a marker to indicate the beginning of the round.

Work 6 rounds in K 2, P 2 rib. In the first round place a marker at the half-way point (64 sts).

Work 5 rounds in garter stitch, then work in st-st for 7 cm, then work pattern as follows:
1st round: *K 1 in M, K 1 in C1*, rep from * to * to end.

2nd round: Work in C1.
3rd round: As 1st round.
   Work 6 rounds in M.
10th round: Work in C2.
11th round: *K 1 in M, K1 in C2*, rep from * to * to end.
   Work 6 rounds in M.
18th round: Work in C3.
19th round: Work in M.
20th round: Work in C3.
   Work 3 rounds in M.
24th round: As 1st round.
25th round: Work in M.
26th and 27th rounds: Work in C1.
28th round: Work in M.

Back and sleeves

Break off M and join in C4. Work to marker, then invisibly cast on 32 sts.
1st row: K 8, P to marker, invisibly cast on 32 sts (128 sts). Thread remaining sts onto a length of left-over yarn.
2nd row: K in C2.
3rd row: Using C4, K 8, P 112, K 8.
4th row: *K 1 in C2, K 1 in C4*, rep from * to * to end.
5th row: As 3rd row.
6th row: K in C4.
7th row: As 3rd row.
8th row: K in C3.
9th row: *(K 1 in C3, K 1 in C 4) 4 times*, (P 1 in C 3, P 1 in C 4) 48 times, rep from * to *.
10th row: K in C 3.
11th row: As 3rd row.
12th row: K in C4.
13th row: Using C1, K 8, P 96, K 8.
14th row: K in C1.
15th row: *(K 1 in C1, K 1 in C4) 4 times*, (P 1 in C1, P 1 in C4) to last 8 sts, rep from * to *.
16th row: K in C4.

17th row: As 3rd row.
18th row: K in C4.
19th row: As 3rd row.
20th row: K in C2.
21st row: As 3rd row.
22nd row: K in C4.
23rd row: Using C3, K 8, P 112, K 8.
24th row: *K 1 in C3, K 1 in C4*, rep from * to * to end.
25th row: *(K 1 in C3, K 1 in C4) 4 times*, (P 1 in C3, P 1 in C4) to last 8 sts, rep from * to *.
26th row: K in C3.
27th row: As 3rd row.
28th row: K in C4.

Rep 27th and 28th rows twice.

Thread first 53 sts onto a length of left-over yarn, place next 22 sts on stitch-holder, then thread last 53 sts onto a length of left-over yarn.

Front and sleeves

Replace front body sts on circular needle. Using C4, work across front sts then pick up 32 sts from invisible casting on of right sleeve. Work back to end of row and pick up 32 from invisible casting on of left sleeve.

Work the left front as follows:

1st row: Using C2, K 72, turn. Complete the left front on these sts.
2nd row: *(K 1 in C4, K 1 in C2) 4 times*, (P 1 in C4, P 1 in C2) to last 8 sts, rep from * to *.

Working stripes as for back and working the first and last 8 sts of each row in garter st, work 12 more rows.

Next row: Work to last 12 sts, place these sts on a stitch-holder.

Continue working stripes as for back, decreasing 1 st at neck edge in every alternate row 4 times (56 sts).

Work 7 rows without shaping.

Place left back shoulder and sleeve sts on a spare needle and join front and back sts together by one of the methods described in the Joining Shoulders section of Special Techniques on page 12.

Join in yarn at centre front and pick up 4 sts from base of centre band. Complete right front to correspond.

Neckband

Using 4mm double-pointed needles and C4, knit up 12 sts from right front stitch-holder. Pick up 12 sts evenly along right front, knit 22 sts from back neck stitch-holder, then pick up 12 sts along left front and knit 12 sts from left front stitch-holder (58 sts).

Work 4 rows in garter st.
Next row: K to last 5 sts, yfwd, K 2 tog, K 3.

Work 4 more rows in garter st. Cast off loosely.

Making up

Darn in loose ends. Sew on button. Press if desired.

T-shaped Sweater or Jacket

First make a tension sample (see page 10) and take measurements (see page 11). If the garment is for a baby, allow room for growth. For an adult, take off 5 cm from the sleeve measurement to allow for stretching.

Body

From the chest or hip measurement (whichever is the larger), calculate the number of sts required. For a baby's sweater, use a 60 cm or 40 cm circular needle, or if there are not enough sts for a circular needle, use a set of 4 double-pointed needles.

Sweater: Cast on the required number of sts, making sure that there is no twist in the casting on. Work the basque in rib or a combination of rib and garter st. If you are using K 2, P 2 rib make sure that the number of sts is divisible by 4.

Work in rounds until the body is the desired length to the armhole.

Jacket: Add a sufficient number of sts to the casting on to allow for an overlapping band and work in rows, working these extra sts in garter st, working buttonholes at regular intervals.

Back and sleeves

Calculate the number of sts required for the sleeve length. Work half the body sts then invisibly cast on the calculated number of sleeve sts. Thread the rest of the body sts onto a length of left-over yarn. Work back across sleeve and body sts and invisibly cast on another lot of sleeve sts.

Continue working in rows until the sleeve measures half the upper arm measurement, working the first and last few sts of each row in garter st.

Next calculate the number of sts required for the width of the back neck. Subtract this number from the number of sts on the needle and divide the result by 2. Place this number of sts onto a length of left-over yarn, then place the back neck sts onto a stitch holder. Place the remaining sts on another length of left-over yarn.

Front and sleeves

Sweater: Replace front body sts on needle, join in yarn at end of sleeve and work across, picking up sleeve sts from invisible casting on.

Decide how many sts you wish to have for front opening band. Work to centre front, then work the number of front opening band sts. Continue working on these sts, working front band and cuff sts in garter st, until front is approximately half the length of the back.

Leave front neck opening sts on a stitch-holder. This should be a little more than half the number of back neck sts. Shape the neckline by decreasing 1 st every alternate row. Work the last few rows without shaping, then join the front and back shoulder and sleeve sts together using one of the methods given in the Joining Shoulders section of Special Techniques on page 12.

Join yarn at centre front. Pick up the front opening band sts from the bottom of the band and work right front to correspond.

Jacket: Work as for sweater, but work the two sides of the front separately, continuing to work the garter st edging. Work front without shaping until the shoulder is reached.

Shoulder and sleeve shaping

For an adult garment, the shoulder and sleeve may be shaped at the top edge. In this case, work the back and sleeves section only until the sleeve measures half the wrist measurement. The top of the sleeve may now be shaped by working in steps. Subtract the number of rows in half the wrist from the number of rows in half the upper arm and divide the result by 2. The number of sts in each step will then be the number of sleeve sts divided by the number of steps. Work these steps as short rows, working to the calculated number of sts in each step from the end of the sleeve, turning (see page 11) and working to the same point on the other sleeve. Continue working the steps in this manner until the sleeve is completed.

Shape the front and sleeves to correspond and join the sts together as described above.

Sweater neckband

Knit sts from right front stitch-holder, pick up 1 st for every row up right side of neck, knit sts from back neck stitch-holder, pick up corresponding number of sts along left side of neck, then knit sts from left front stitch-holder.

Work neckband to desired width in garter st, working a buttonhole in the middle row on the left front. Cast off loosely.

Jacket neck and collar

For a wide collar on the jacket, continue working on the front and back neck sts in your chosen stitch pattern for about 12 cm, working the front edges in garter st as before, then work approximately 5 cm in garter st. Cast off.

Making up

Darn in loose ends.

Sweater: Sew on button.

Jacket: Work two rows of double crochet around all edges. Sew on buttons.
Press if desired.

Sideways-knitted Vest

Illustrated on page 88

This vest features a peaked front, pockets and a four-colour striped pattern on each side. It is worked sideways, commencing at the underarm, in check stitch and garter stitch.

Fits chest size (cm)

A	B	C	D
85	90	**95**	100

Measures (cm)

95	100	105	110

Materials

  50 gm balls of 5-ply yarn
  Main colour (M): **5**: 5: **6**: 6 balls
  1 ball each of 4 contrasting colours (C1, C2, C3 and C4)
  80 cm circular needle and pair of straight needles in size 3.75 mm
  5 small buttons
  Small quantity of left-over yarn

Tension

30 sts and 44 rows to 10 cm, measured over check stitch.

Check stitch

1st round: (K 2, P 2) to end.
2nd and 3rd rounds: K the K sts and P the P sts as they present.
4th round: P the K sts and K the P sts as they present.
5th and 6th rounds: As 2nd round.

INSTRUCTIONS

The work begins at the left back end of the underarm.

Using the circular needle and M, invisibly cast on **58**: 60: **60**: 64 sts. Working in check st, work 1 row, then decrease 1 st at beginning of next and every alternate row 4 times (**50**: 52: **52**: 56 sts).

Work **50**: 56: **64**: 72 more rows in check st, then inc 1 st at each end of next and every alternate row 4 times (**66**: 68: **68**: 72 sts).

Work 1 row in check st.

Left armhole

1st row: K 1, inc 1, K to end, cast on **105**: 107: **107**: 105 sts, knit up **58**: 60: **60**: 64 sts from invisible casting on (**230**: 236: **236**: 242 sts).

Work 6 rows in garter st, increasing as before in every alternate row on front.

Left striped panel and pocket

Before commencing this section, wind off a separate quantity of yarn from each contrasting ball.
1st row: Using C1, K **124**: 130: **130**: 136, K 2 in C2, K 2 in C1, K 2 in C2, K 36 in C1, K 2 in C2, K 2 in C 1, K 2 in C 2, K 16, PM, K 30. Using the second ball of C1 and C2 and a straight needle, beginning at the marker, pick up 30 sts from last garter st ridge, working these sts as follows: K 16 in C1, K 2 in C2, K 2 in C1, K 2 in C2, K 8 in C1. This point is the bottom of the pocket. Wind yarn around yarn from circular needle and work to end of row in C1 with straight needle.
2nd row: Using C1, K 1, inc 1, K to bottom of pocket. Continuing on straight needle, K 8 in C1, K 2 in C2, K 2 in C1, K 2 in C2, K in C1 to end of straight needle. Return to circular needle at bottom of pocket and K 46 in C1, K 2 in C2, K 2 in C1, K

2 in C2, K 36 in C1, K 2 in C2, K 2 in C 1, K 2 in C2, K to end in C1.

3rd row: Using C2, K **120**: 126: **126**: 132, *(K 2 in C3, K 2 in C2) 3 times, K 2 in C3*, K 28 in C2, rep from * to *, K 46 in C2. Return to straight needle. K 12 in C2, rep from * to *, K 4 in C2. Wind yarn around yarn from circular needle and work to end of row in C2 with straight needle.

4th row: Using C2, K 1, inc 1, K to bottom of pocket. Continuing on straight needle, K 4 in C2, *(K 2 in C3, K 2 in C2) 3 times, K 2 in C3*, K in C2 to end of straight needle. Return to circular needle at bottom of pocket and K 42 in C1, rep from * to *, K 28 in C1, rep from * to *, K to end in C2.

5th row: Using C3, K **116**: 122: **122**: 128, *(K 2 in M, K 2 in C3) 5 times, K 2 in M*, K 20 in C3, rep from * to *, K 38 in C3. Return to straight needle. K 8 in C3, (K 2 in M, K 2 in C3) 4 times, K 2 in M, K 4 in C3. Wind yarn around yarn from circular needle and work to end of row in C3 with straight needle.

6th row: Using C3, K 1, inc 1, K to bottom of pocket. Continuing on straight needle, K 4 in C3, *(K 2 in M, K 2 in C3) 4 times, K 2 in M*, K in C3 to end of straight needle. Return to circular needle at bottom of pocket and K 38 in C3, *(K 2 in M, K 2 in C3) 5 times, K 2 in M* , rep from * to *, K 20 in C3, rep from * to *, K to end in C2.

7th row: Using M, K **116**: 122: **122**: 128, *(K 2 in C2, K 2 in M) 5 times, K 2 in C2*, K 20 in M, rep from * to *, K 38 in M. Return to straight needle. K 8 in M, (K 2 in C2, K 2 in M) 4 times, K 2 in C2, K 4 in M. Wind yarn around yarn from circular needle and work to end of row in M with straight needle.

8th row: Using M, K 1, inc 1, K to bottom of pocket. Continuing on straight needle, K 4 in M, (K 2 in C2, K 2 in M) 4 times, K 2 in C2, K in M to end of straight needle. Return to circular needle at bottom of pocket and K 38 in M, *(K 2 in C2, K 2 in M) 5 times, K 2 in C2*, rep from * to *, K 20 in M, rep from * to *, K to end in M.

9th row: Using C2, K **112**: 118: **118**: 124, *(K 2 in C4, K 2 in C2) 7 times, K 2 in C4*, K 12 in C2, rep from * to *, K 34 in C2. Return to straight needle. K 4 in C2, (K 2 in C4, K 2 in C2) 6 times, K 2 in C4. Wind yarn around yarn from circular needle and work to end of row in C2 with straight needle.

10th row: Using C2, K 1, inc 1, K to bottom of pocket. Continuing on straight needle, (K 2 in C4, K 2 in C2) 6 times, K 2 in C4, K in C2 to end of straight needle. Return to circular needle at bottom of pocket and K 34 in C2, *(K 2 in C4, K 2 in C2) 7 times, K 2 in C4*, rep from * to *, K 12 in C2, rep from * to *, K to end in C2.

11th row: Using C4, K **112**: 118: **118**: 124, *(K 2 in C1, K 2 in C4) 7 times, K 2 in C1*, K 12 in C4, rep from * to *, K 34 in C4. Return to straight needle.

K 4 in C4, (K 2 in C1, K 2 in C4) 6 times, K 2 in C1. Wind yarn around yarn from circular needle and work to end of row in C4 with straight needle.

12th row: Using C4, K 1, inc 1, K to bottom of pocket. Continuing on straight needle, (K 2 in C1, K 2 in C4) 6 times, K 2 in C1, K in C4 to end of straight needle. Return to circular needle at bottom of pocket and K 34 in C4, *(K 2 in C1, K 2 in C4) 7 times, K 2 in C1*, rep from * to *, K 12 in C4, rep from * to *, K to end in C4.

13th row: Using C1, K **112**: 118: **118**: 124, *(K 2 in M, K 2 in C1) 7 times, K 2 in M*, K 12 in C1, rep from * to *, K 34 in M. Return to straight needle. K 4 in C1, (K 2 in M, K 2 in C1) 6 times, K 2 in M. Wind yarn around yarn from circular needle and work to end of row in C1 with straight needle.

14th row: Using C1, K 1, inc 1, K to bottom of pocket. Continuing on straight needle, (K 2 in M, K 2 in C1) 6 times, K 2 in M, K in C1 to end of straight needle. Return to circular needle at bottom of pocket and K 34 in C1, *(K 2 in M, K 2 in C1) 7 times, K 2 in M*, rep from * to *, K 12 in C1, rep from * to *, K to end in C1.

15th row: Using M, K to bottom of pocket. Return to straight needle and K pocket sts in M. Wind yarn around yarn from circular needle and work to end of row in M.

16th row: Using M, K to bottom of pocket. Continuing on straight needle, work in M to end of pocket. Return to circular needle. Using M, K to end (**240**: 246: **246**: 252 sts).

Work 14 more rows in similar manner, decreasing 1 st at front edge in alternate rows instead of increasing, and working colour pattern as follows: 1st and 2nd rows, C2 and M; 3rd and 4th rows, C3 and C2; 5th and 6th rows, C1 and C3; 7th and 8th rows, M and C1; 9th and 10th rows, C2 and M; 11th and 12th rows, C4 and C2; 13th and 14th rows, C1 and C4.

Continuing to decrease on front edge as before, change to M and work 5 rows in garter st, working upper and lower pocket sts together in 1st row (**231**: 237: **237**: 243 sts).

Left front shaping

Continue the work in check st.

1st row: Work **110**: 113: **113**: 116 in check st, PM, work to end.

2nd row: Decrease 1 st, work to last 4 sts, turn.

3rd row: Work to end.

Rep 2nd and 3rd rows 6 times.

15th row: Work to marker in garter st.

Thread **107**: 110: **110**: 113 sts (to marker) on a length of left-over yarn.

Back

Using M, work **56**: 60: **62**: 66 rows in check st.

Right front shaping

At end of last row of back, invisibly cast on **107**: 110: **110**: 113 sts. Continue work in check st.
1st row: K 1, inc 1, work **50**: 53: **53**: 56, turn.
2nd row: Work to end.
3rd row: K 1, inc 1, work **54**: 57: **57**: 60, turn.
4th row: Work to end.

Continue in this manner, in every alternate row increasing 1 st at lower edge and knitting up 4 more sts at upper edge, until all cast-on sts are knitted up.

Right striped panel and pocket

Continue increasing at lower front edge as before. Work 5 rows in garter st across front and back, then work striped panel and pocket to correspond with left front, reversing colour pattern (1st and 2nd rows, C1 and C4; 2nd and 3rd rows, C4 and C2, and so on).

Continuing to decrease at lower front edge, work 6 rows in M in garter st.

Right armhole

Work **58**: 60: **60**: 64 sts in check st, cast off **105**: 107: **107**: 105, work to end in check st. Complete the underarm on these sts.

Working in check st, decrease 1 st at each end of next and alternate rows 4 times, then work **50**: 56: **64**: 72 more rows in check st.

Inc at armhole edge in next and alternate rows 4 times. Work 1 row.

Place underarm and back sts side by side. Cast sts off together, using method 2(a) for joining shoulders in on page 12.

Band

With right side facing and M, beginning at lower edge of right front, knit up sts from invisible casting on. Pick up **38**: 40: **41**: 44 sts along edge of back neck, then knit up sts from length of yarn on left front.
1st row: K.
2nd row: K 4, cast off 2 for buttonhole. Work 4 more buttonholes evenly spaced between bottom edge and beginning of neck shaping (see page 14).
3rd row: K to 1st buttonhole. Cast on 2 sts over each buttonhole. K to end.

Work 5 more rows in garter st. Cast off.

Making up

Darn in loose ends. Sew on buttons. Do not press.

Sideways-knitted Vest

First make a tension sample (see page 10). If you intend to use a stitch pattern instead of stocking st (e.g. check st as in the preceding pattern), make your sample in this stitch. Next take the following measurements: chest (add about 5 or 6 cm to the actual measurement), shoulders (a narrower measurement than you would use for a sweater), armhole (a looser measurement for a deeper armhole), and length from neck to waist.

Begin the work at the back of the left armhole. Calculate the number of sts to cast on as follows: Divide two-thirds of the armhole measurement by 2 and subtract the result from the length from neck to waist. Convert this number into sts (calculated from your tension sample).

Next calculate the underarm rows. Convert one-third of the armhole measurement into rows. Divide the result by 5 to obtain the number of decreases in the armhole shaping.

Invisibly cast on the calculated number of sts and work in your chosen background st, decreasing 1 st at the beginning of every alternate row until you have taken off the calculated number of decreases.

Multiply the number of rows worked by 3 and work this number of rows without shaping.

Next work the front armhole slope by increasing to correspond with the decreases on the back, at the same time increasing in each alternate row at the lower end to begin the shaping for the front peaks.

Convert two-thirds of the armhole measurement into sts from your tension sample and cast on this number of sts. Knit up the invisibly cast on sts and work the front and back of the left shoulder together.

A few rows may now be worked in garter st for the armhole border. If you wish to add a ribbed border later, work on in your chosen stitch pattern.

Left shoulder

The width of the left shoulder should be approximately one-third of the shoulder measurement. This may be worked in a different stitch pattern and/or with contrasting colours. If a different stitch pattern is to be used, work another tension sample to estimate the number of rows required for the shoulder measurement.

The increases at the lower front edge are continued until the centre of the shoulder side is reached, then corresponding decreases are worked from that point to the last row of the front.
Note: If pockets are desired, see pattern for method (page 104).

Left front shaping

Starting with a right side row, work the lower back and half the armhole sts then place a marker at that point.

Next calculate the front shaping. This should end at a point approximately level with the underarm. From your row tension, calculate the number of rows required for the back neck measurement. This will be the shoulder measurement minus twice the previously calculated shoulder side measurement. You will need half this number of rows for the neck shaping.

Divide the number of rows in the neck shaping by 2 to obtain the number of steps in the shaping. Then divide the number of sts in the shaped edge by the number of steps to obtain the number of sts in each step. If the number does not divide evenly, make up the difference on the last step.

Work the shaping in short rows while continuing the shaping at lower edge as before. Work to the calculated number of sts in the steps before the marker, turn and work to end of row. Continue in this manner until you have reached the end of the shaping, then work all the front sts to the end of the row at the back. Thread the front sts onto a length of left-over yarn.

Centre back

Work back to the marker, then work the required number of rows for the back neck measurement, ending at the neck end of the row.

Right front shaping

Invisibly cast on the number of sts to correspond with the left front. Work the neck shaping to correspond with the left front, ending at the neck edge. At the same time increase at the lower edge in every alternate row to correspond with the left front.

Right shoulder

Work to correspond with left shoulder, shaping lower edge in alternate rows.

When the shoulder side is completed, cast off the armhole sts and work the right underarm to correspond with the left, shaping at both ends of front section and at armhole end of back.

When the underarm section is completed, the remaining sts may be joined to the invisible casting on either by grafting or by one of the methods given for joining shoulders on page 12.

Front band

With right side of work facing and starting at lower edge of right front, knit up sts from invisible casting on, pick up 2 sts for every 3 rows across back neck, then knit up sts from length of left-over yarn.

Work band either in garter st or in rib, working buttonholes on right front for a woman or left front for a man.

Ribbed bands may also be worked around the armholes.

Making up

Darn in loose ends. Sew on buttons. Press if desired.

Ribbed Skirt

Illustrated on page 88

This skirt will team well with the vest in the preceding pattern. It is so simple that an exact pattern is not necessary. The original was worked in 8-ply wool on 4 mm needles.

The first step is to take the hip measurement. This should be taken loosely over the widest part of the hip.

Next make a tension sample in your chosen yarn. Cast on about 100 sts and work approximately 10 cm in K 4, P 2 rib.

Measure the width of the sample, slightly stretched, and calculate from it the number of sts required for your hip measurement. Adjust this number of sts to a multiple of six.

Using an 80 cm circular needle, cast on the calculated number of sts by the thumb method (taking care that there is no twist in the casting on) and work in K 4, P 2 rib until the skirt is the required length.

Eyelet round: *yfwd, sl 1, K 1, psso, K 2 tog, yfwd, P 2*, rep from * to * to end of round.

Rib 1 round, then cast off loosely in rib.

Thread elastic, a crocheted chain or twisted cord long enough to tie around the waist through the eyelets.

Index